HOW TO SET UP
the Best Sounding Banjo

ISBN 0-7935-8998-3

7777 W. BLUEMOUND RD. P.O. BOX 13819 MILWAUKEE, WI 53213

Visit Hal Leonard Online at
www.halleonard.com

How often have you heard someone say "I've always loved the sound of a banjo?" The brilliant style and tone introduced by Earl Scruggs in the 1940s has inspired hundreds of thousands of people worldwide to learn to make that evocative sound.

Now, over 50 years later, here is the first book to describe, thoroughly and authoritatively, how the banjo produces sound and how to customize it to a player's tastes. Roger Siminoff's years of hands-on experience and his knack for clear explanation help us follow banjo tone all the way from the strings and tone chamber to our inner ears.

This long-overdue information will be a valuable resource for every banjo player. Thanks, Roger!

Pete Wernick

Pete Wernick
Niwot, Colorado

About the Author

Roger H. Siminoff has been designing, building, playing, and researching musical instruments for more than 40 years. The combination of these talents, coupled with his love of writing, has made Siminoff one of America's foremost authorities on string instruments and their design, a leading music journalist, and a highly respected inventor.

Born in 1940 in Newark, New Jersey, Siminoff showed an early interest in things both musical and mechanical. As a teenager, one of Roger's first lutherie projects was a pedal steel guitar with linkage assembled from model airplane parts. The steel guitar was followed by a complete five-string banjo after which he produced numerous five-string necks to convert four-string instruments to the popular bluegrass models.

By the early 1960s Roger was building custom banjo necks and parts for musicians in the New York metropolitan area. And, before the end of the decade, his mail-order parts business, Siminoff Banjos, was providing banjo and mandolin parts to instrument makers in every part of the world. Siminoff Banjos continued producing components and answering the needs of luthiers until 1985.

Having branched out into the building of mandolins in early 1970, Siminoff conceived and built special carving machines to do the exact shaping of instrument necks, and of mandolin top and back plates. To bend wood for banjo rims and mandolin sides he developed a unique steam chamber long enough to roll a 12' length of 1/4" maple into a single seamless banjo rim. By 1973, he had developed a multi-axis truss rod system to counteract the forces of string tension on musical instrument necks. For this design, he was awarded a U.S. Patent in 1974, and later licensed the patent to Gibson Incorporated.

After attending Parsons School of Design in New York City where he majored in industrial design, Roger founded a graphic arts company in New Jersey that specialized in photography, art and design services, and printing. With creative facilities readily available to him, Siminoff channeled his banjo expertise into writing an instruction book for bluegrass banjo playing (*5-String Banjo, Bluegrass Style*, 1972). The publication quickly became a success, and a bound-in offer triggered the response for what was to follow: the creation of a monthly music magazine that focused on bluegrass and old-time country music. In February 1974, *Pickin' Magazine* made its debut. Within two years, it was hailed as the most influential publication of its kind.

By mid 1975, as *Pickin'* was growing in the background, Roger had several other musical designs in progress. These included the invention of a guitar tuning knob with a fold-out fast-wind crank for which he was granted a U.S. Patent and several foreign patents. The knob, dubbed the "CRANK," has been licensed to Gibson and to Schaller (W. Germany), a world renowned manufacturer of tuning machines. A unique nut, with adjustable-action supports for each string, won Siminoff another U.S. Patent and subsequently was licensed to Dunlop Manufacturing. Then, his frustrations at the inconvenience of changing strings won him a few more patents; he developed two methods to change instruments strings without cutting, twisting, or knotting them. One design, a string with a special pin at its peghead end, was licensed to Gibson under the name "GRABBERS."

In early 1984, Roger was granted another U.S. Patent, this one for an unusual modular guitar. It features interlocking parts that permit a musician to snap together an instrument to suit his or her tastes in much the same way a photographer might assemble camera bodies and lenses. Two years later, another patent followed, this one for a universal mounting system for tuning machines. Today, several other music-related designs are awaiting their turn for further development on the Siminoff workbench.

As a consultant to Gibson, Roger assisted in reissuing several instruments originally produced by the Company in its earlier years. Among these were the Earl Scruggs model banjo (a replica of Scruggs' personal Gibson Granada), and the reintroduction of the famed F-5 mandolin as first produced by Gibson in the mid 1920's. The reissue, dubbed the F-5L after its creator Lloyd Loar, has been enthusiastically received since making its successful "comeback" in June of 1978.

Consulting for several other instrument manufacturers, Siminoff has been responsible for the development of special hand-finishing techniques, improved structural and acoustical designs, production machining and pattern-carving of wood parts, string winding and tensioning technology, and compatibility "tuning" of the acoustic properties for production instruments.

Siminoff has authored several hundred articles on instrument construction and repair, musical acoustics, performers, and the history and craftsmanship of musical instruments. His research and writings on the life and work of both Orville Gibson and Lloyd Loar have made him a highly respected expert on these renowned artisans.

In 1979, Roger was invited to join GPI Publications in Cupertino, California, to launch *FRETS Magazine.* As the magazine's founding editor, Roger helped build *FRETS* into a viable acoustic music publication, boasting an unprecedented international circulation of more than 30,000 readers within a two-and-a-half year period.

In 1988, the magic of computers lured Siminoff in another direction where he sought to understand the contribution this technology could make to the world of music and publishing.

When away from computers and instruments, Roger can be found on his sailboat with, of course, bluegrass music blending with the sound of the wind.

But nothing has substituted his interest in music. His shop boasts many in-progress instruments, and his diet still includes consulting to the major manufacturers, and articles and texts on music related themes keep pouring from his computer.

ALSO BY ROGER SIMINOFF

Constructing a Bluegrass Mandolin
(Hal Leonard Publishing)

Constructing a 5-String Banjo
(Hal Leonard Publishing)

Constructing a Solid Body Guitar
(Hal Leonard Publishing)

The Gibson Authoritative Guide to Musical Strings
(Gibson Strings & Accessories)

With great appreciation to
my wife Mattee for her support and editing talent.

Cover Photography
Andrew Siminoff

Photography
Roger Siminoff

Illustrations
Peggy Shea

This book is dedicated
to the magical musical gifts of
Earl Scruggs and Pete Seeger

and to the memory of
Hub Nitchie, Richard Schneider, and James Rickard

Contents

Preface

I'm not sure whether it is pride, the pleasure of hearing the music we create, or just plain human nature that makes musicians strive to play better. In any case, it brings about an interesting cycle: practice brings us closer to perfection and stimulates our joy of playing, which, in turn stimulates the desire to practice. We enjoy the interaction with our instrument, the quality of its voice, the ability to bring it alive, the intricacy of manipulating its strings, and the oneness felt when the player and the instrument are in harmony.

As our musical skills develop, it is common to desire the ideal instrument, seeking better attributes that may include: cosmetics, volume, tone, balance, feel, and in some cases, *the* recognized brand. On the other hand, should one be so inclined, the existing instrument can be modified to advance it closer to perfection. Developing our musical skills and improving our instrument's acoustic performance are both very rewarding experiences.

The banjo offers great exploratory options and experimental opportunities. It can be completely disassembled in less than an hour, and re-assembled just as quickly. There are numerous replacement parts and tons of adjustments, the combinations of which can be tested again and again. When all is said and done, the expectation of re-assembly is that the instrument will be one step closer to the desired point of perfection. At the very least, the experience derived from the mechanical relationship with the instrument brings us closer to a philosophical perfection, and makes both it and us *feel* better.

No matter how well made, no two instruments of the same model will sound exactly the same. Differences in wood, hardware, fit, finish, and age play a major role in how the instrument sounds. Some things can be changed, others cannot. And, there are those things that are easy to remedy and others that require skilled luthierie. Age is one of those interesting "cannot change" components. As my good friend Mike Longworth of Martin Guitars used to say, "we just haven't found a way to make a *new* instrument that's 50 years old!" He's right. But, there is a lot we can do to improve its output.

In this book I will explain how your banjo works and how to achieve the best acoustical dynamics from it. Even if you choose to change only the strings, it is my hope that you will have a better understanding of how all components in your banjo work.

Many of the images in this book and much of the discussion centers around Gibson-style banjos — an outcome of this brand's high visibility and popularity. This is not intended to single out this instrument over any other. There are many excellent manufacturers producing banjos today. Suffice it to say that with the exception of dowel-stick neck attachments, all attributes and techniques expressed in this text can be related to all banjo makes and models.

So, if you choose to explore the world of opportunities waiting for you in your banjo case, this book is your roadmap. Have fun.

Roger Siminoff

SOME THINGS TO CONSIDER

1. In musical acoustics, we talk about a "coupled system" suggesting that each element has a relationship to every other element in the instrument. This implies that changing one component might have an affect on one or several other components. While I have attempted to cross-reference these whenever possible, it is recommended that you spend time reading the entire text before making any changes to your banjo. Approach the process holistically, rather than piecemeal.

2. In this text, we will go through the numerous facets of the banjo, from peghead to tailpiece, from strings to resonator. I do not suggest that you personally make every adjustment. Some of the suggestions require the experience of a skilled luthier, others you can do yourself. Only do what you think you can do safely or without causing irreparable damage.

3. Two checklists are provided at the end of the text. The first offers a list of items that affect the banjo's tone and amplitude, listed from most important or most significant to least. The second list contains the same information but the list is ranked from easiest to most difficult to implement.

4. Bear in mind that altering a new instrument may adversely affect the manufacturer's warranty.

PLEASE NOTE
The reader assumes full responsibility for changes made to the instrument and agrees to hold Roger H. Siminoff and Hal Leonard Corporation harmless from the outcome of any alterations or adjustments made from or implied by this text.

Introduction

OVERVIEW: A HISTORY OF THE BANJO

Portable balladeer instruments have roots back to the days of the Crusaders when numerous handcrafted, reed or finger played, fretted and fretless, wood- and skin-covered instruments lead from one creative development to another. Plucked instruments, the sounds they produce, and the ballads through which they communicate have been an inextricable part of human societies and cultures worldwide as far back as we can study.

While the popular view supports a notion that the banjo is a true American instrument, history suggests that the instrument dates back to Africa, and possibly beyond. Some references to stringed, skinned-head, tack-head instruments appear in print as early as 1790.

The banjo's closest European cousin is the Arabian *rebab* which grew into three other families: the *rebec, fidula,* and *vielle.* Other relatives were the *lute* of Persia, deriving its name and shape from the Arabic word *Al'ud* ("wood"), and a plucked zither called the *psaltery* (which could also be played with small mallets like our hammered dulcimer), which also came from Persia, although its name was derived from Greece.

It is believed that black slaves brought one of these musical ancestors to the United States from Africa in the early 1700s. By 1785 the banjo had achieved popularity, and in that year Thomas Jefferson wrote in his *Notes on the State of Virginia* that the "banjar" was the "principal musical instrument of the American Negroes." Around 1830, Joel Walker Sweeney, a popular Virginia musician, added a fifth or drone string to the four-string banjo. While five-string instruments were not new, per se, the earlier versions provided for all strings to be fretted and Sweeney's fifth string was not. Whether Sweeney's attraction was to the constant drone note of the bagpipes and other early instruments, or whether he was just experimenting for a new sound will never be known. What does remain is the development of a new instrument, a robust growth of idioms and styles, and the ensuing volumes of lyrical treasures.

Today's banjos with their highly mechanical structures, can attribute their contemporary development to such heralded American manufacturers as Bacon & Day, Paramount, Lange, Vega, Crown, Orpheum, Fairbanks, S.S. Stewart, and Gibson. And, one cannot forget the thousands of plastic-bodied Kay and Harmony banjos that helped fuel the fire — both literally and figuratively.

Most of the development occurred at the turn of the century as banjo bands were the popular entertainment highlight of the day. For almost three decades the instrument flourished and was produced in large numbers in a wide variety of models to suit the playing styles of virtually all string-instrument performers and to provide the tone color of everything from big voices to little. Thus, it was not unusual to find models of banjos designated as bass, tenor, plectrum, 5-string (or "regular banjo"), 6-string (for guitar tuning), ukulele, mandolin, and the tiny 4-string piccolo versions.

Fig. 1-1. The "Gibsonians" were sponsored by Gibson and featured (from left): Dorothy Crane, Fisher Shipp (Lloyd Loar's first wife), Lloyd A. Loar, James H. Johnstone (holding Lloyd's TB-5), Nell VerCies, and Lucille Campbell.

Throughout this period, the main features of the instrument were a natural-skin thin-membrane round soundboard (head) held in tension by a ring tightened by metal brackets, a wood rim of various constructions, some form of sound ring or tone chamber, a neck attached with a wooden alignment dowel or adjustable metal rods, and an open back or detachable closure (resonator).

The unique constructions offered by each of the manufacturers brought with them an equally unique sound. With all the diversity of tones, three main tone-colors or "tambres" rang true and have sustained to this day: open-back 5-string folk banjos, resonated four-string Dixieland tenor and plectrum banjos, and the ever popular five-string bluegrass banjos. While a broad list of names comes to mind, most would agree that these instrument groups, in order, were rocketed to popularity by the creative talents of such great artisans as Pete Seeger, Eddy Peabody, and Earl Scruggs.

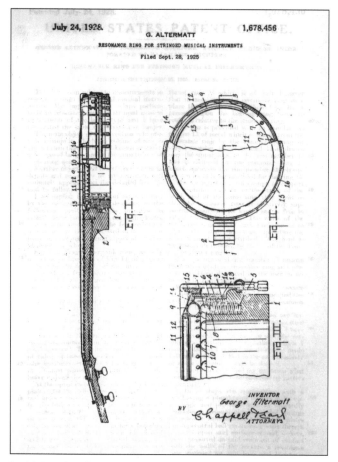

Fig. 1-2. Banjo design became a science in the early '20s. George Altermatt described his ideas for the ball-bearing tone chamber in this 1925 patent.

Fig. 1-4. Elaborately colored and adorned, the high-end banjo models were designed to catch the listener's eye as well as ear.

Fig. 1-3. Skin heads came in many models based on surface, thickness, and skin quality, including the Jos. Rogers shown above.

Fig. 1-5. B&D hand engraved both wood and metal parts. Each instrument was a unique piece of art.

The early soundboards, or "heads," were made of calfskin, a membrane that imparted a warm and rich tone to the instrument. Skin heads were also highly susceptible to changes in humidity and were, for most musicians, a nightmare to install. As head makers like Jos B. Rogers Jr. sought to improve their product for banjos and drums alike, a material called Mylar emerged from technological efforts associated with World War II. Mylar was a new plastic with the strength and durability beyond that of natural skin, and a molecular structure that did not change with the weather.

At the turn of the century, banjo bands had sprung up everywhere, with many being sponsored by manufacturers of musical instruments. At that period, S.S. Stewart, Paramount, Fairbanks, Vega, and Bacon & Day were the major providers of banjos, and competition for banjo sales was fierce. In 1917, the Gibson Mandolin-Guitar Co. of Kalamazoo, Michigan, announced a line of banjos with a revolutionary ball-bearing tone tube. Equally important to Gibson's prowess in instrument development, the company was a very aggressive marketeer and it, too, supported numerous mandolin and banjo bands to help spread the Gibson name.

The Roaring '20s was a popular time for the banjo. During the next few decades, the race was on for banjo technology, as Gibson announced new developments every two or three months. This was a time when accessories flourished, too. Wrist-operated mutes, clip-on bridge mutes, "head lights," hinged resonators, and more were offered to expand the range and feasibility of the banjo in the popular music of the day.

Beyond tone, size, and the number of strings, emerged an even more exciting and time-honored aspect of these wonderful instruments: their artistry. It is difficult to think of another musical instrument so proudly and lavishly adorned with pearl, abalone, gold, silver, chrome, nickel, curly maple, walnut, rosewood, celluloid, marquetry, hand-engraved or plain, multi-layered bindings, purfling, shinny, round, heavy, richly finished, and honored with a plush-lined case.

The banjo was magic — its crystal voice sounding brightly above all others, adding sparkle, drive, snap, and rhythm. The sound was truly unique and everyone cheered the banjo player.

Banjo players are a unique lot, too, and most probably because they share the pleasures associated with such an unusual instrument. What other instrument can you take apart right down to the last screw, and put back together again in the span of an hour?

And, question number two might be "Why?" The answers are plentiful: banjo players share the quest for optimum playing pleasure, easy action, bright clear tones, and good sustain. The banjo allows such experimentation. As in any music idioms, musicians emulate their mentors, and most 5-string bluegrass banjo pickers seek "a banjo that sounds like Earl's."

This book will tell you how to get close. The rest is up to you.

So, let's turn to Chapter 2 and get started . . . good luck!

How It Works

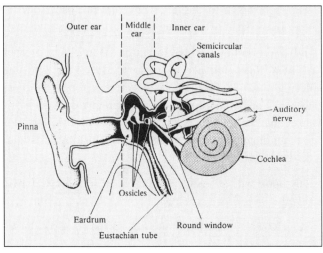

Our appreciation for the sounds of life begin with our ear and the sense of hearing.

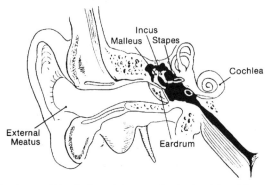

Fig. 2-1. Sound waves which strike the eardrum are transferred to the window of the cochlea through the "ossicles," a set of small bones consisting of the malleus, incus, and stapes.

MOTHER NATURE'S GIFT

A brief description of musical acoustics is in order here, and we would probably be remiss if we did not consider the greatest acoustical instrument of all, the human ear.

Our process of hearing begins with a tunnel called the "auditory meatus," which leads from the world around us to our ear drum or "tympanic membrane." Much like the banjo head, this sensitive little skin is stretched across a round opening (Fig. 2-1), and like the banjo head it has a bridge — actually a little foot connected to the center of the tympanic membrane called the hammer ("malleus"). The hammer is connected to another bone; a very interesting leverage point called the anvil ("incus"), which in turn is connected to a third little bone called the stirrup ("stapes"). Finally, the stirrup is connected to another membrane called the "oval window," which covers a small cone-like space (cochlea) filled with liquid and sensitive nerves.

So, there's the structure, here's how it works: sound waves enter the ear canal and cause the ear drum to vibrate, the hammer (attached to the back of the ear drum) vibrates and leverages on the anvil to force the stirrup to vibrate. The stirrup causes the oval window to vibrate, which sends vibrations through the liquid to those nerves which are sensitive to specific frequencies, and when they are excited, our brain does a quick computation and voila — we hear "sound."

And, as to that very interesting leverage point I told you about... you know how the iris in your eye closes when you are in bright light? Well, the ear makes a similar adjust-ment when you are in a loud environment. To prevent loud noise from damaging the three small bones (the group of three bones is called the "ossicles") or the oval window (which would be *very* painful), after a few seconds of loud noise the anvil turns and changes the mechanical advantage between the stirrup and the hammer. Thus, big vibrations are made smaller on their way to your inner ear — sort of an automatic volume control. Mother Nature is pretty cool, huh?

SOUND PRESSURE

Sound is produced by something vibrating which in turn causes the air around it to vibrate. The air, on its way to your ear, moves in layers of compression and non-compression, or "rarefaction," causing neighboring layers of air to move in similar compression and rarefaction. The movement of air is similar to ripples in a pool of water: each molecule of water doesn't move across the pool, rather each molecule bumps the next and retreats resulting in only the last few molecules striking the shore.

The rate at which air moves is measured in frequency (vibrations per second, today called "Hertz," or "Hz," for short). The average human can hear a frequency range from about 25Hz to about 18,000Hz. The amplitude (loudness) is measured in "sound pressure" on a scale called "dB" (deci-Bels, a logarithmic formula where each 3dB is equal to twice the sound pressure). A few examples of dB are as follows: normal office noise is about 50dB, an acoustic guitar played with a flatpick and measured about three feet away generates about 80dB, and our threshold of pain for sound is about 130dB.

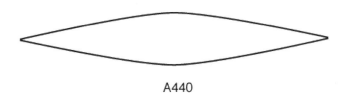

A440

Fig. 2-2. The basic or "fundamental" vibration of a string is the motion it makes when vibrating in one full arc. This is its lowest rate of vibration and is the note to which the string is tuned, in this case, A440.

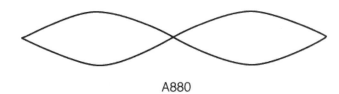

A880

Fig. 2-3. Strings also vibrate in segments or "partials." The second partial, where the string vibrates in halves, creates the note of A880. This note is one octave above the fundamental and is part of the string's whole sound.

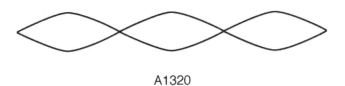

A1320

Fig. 2-4. When an A440 string vibrates in three segments (the third partial), it produces A1320 (three times faster than A440).

A1760

Fig. 2-5. The fourth partial is also heard as part of the string's whole sound. As many as 16 to 18 partials make up the string's whole sound.

SOUNDS FROM INSTRUMENTS

In stringed musical instruments, the strings are the energizers — actually the picks or the bows deliver the initial energy, but more on that in a moment. The energy from the strings excites the soundboard, or "head" in the case of the banjo, to vibrate. When the head vibrates it moves masses of air in front of and behind it, sending soundwaves across the room.

By themselves, the strings have sufficient energy, but lack the surface area (they are too tiny) to move enough air for us to hear them, and thus we need to connect them to something larger like a soundboard (head).

VIBRATION OF STRINGS

While a vibrating string seems simple, the movements it makes are actually quite complex. Strings vibrate in different modes or sections, sometimes vibrating as a whole length of string, sometimes vibrating in halves, or thirds, or fourths, and so on.

When a string — let's say an A string tuned to 440Hz (A440) — vibrates as a whole unit (Fig. 2-2), it produces the "fundamental" or basic note to which the string is tuned, and, in this case, that would be *A440* (440 cycles per second — or more properly: 440Hz). However, that A string will also begin to vibrate in halves producing vibrations which are twice as fast as the fundamental (Fig. 2-3) — a note which is one octave above *A440* at *A880* (fifth octave *A*). It will also vibrate in thirds (Fig. 2-4) producing a note which is a fifth above the *A880*, or sixth octave *E* at *E1320*, and then in fourths (Fig. 2-5) at the next octave, or *A1760*, and so on. These parts of the whole are called "partials," and according to how the string was energized

(plucked, hammered, bowed, etc.) and where it was energized (near the end of the string, in the middle, etc.), the string's overall tone will be comprised of as many as 16 or 18 different partials within the whole tone. That is, the overall tone of a string you hear being played is comprised of many discrete tones. How much of overall tone can the human ear can detect? That depends on the amplitude (loudness) and frequency (must be within the human range) of each of the partials.

The partials, and more specifically, the combinations of partials and their relative amplitude (loudness), give the string its tambre or "color." Typically, even-numbered partials (2nd, 4th, and so on) produce warmer tones than odd-numbered partials. Thus, a string which is played or picked such that its odd partials have greater amplitude than its even-numbered ones, will be brighter than one with greater amplitude on its even-numbered partials.

Soundboards vibrate in modes as well, and we will learn in *Chapter 5, Bridges,* that the position of the bridge on the soundboard will play as important a role in the tambre of the instrument as where the string is picked.

One of the reasons various string instruments sound different from each other is because both the *methods, durations,* and *locations* of attack excite different partials on different instruments. For *method* and *duration,* consider picked vs bowed, hammered vs strummed, plastic flatpicks vs metal fingerpicks, and so on. And, for *location,* consider near the bridge, further from the bridge, and near the neck heel. All of these combinations can produce very different sounds from the identical string and instrument.

Some instruments are designed to precisely control the location of attack in order to maintain equal tambre or tonal quality from string to string. On high-quality pianos, for example, the "harp" and bridges are designed so that the hammers strike each string at a point that is 1/7th of the string's length. On fretted instruments, we learn that we can achieve different tambre when playing near the bridge (bright) or close to the neck (warm, mellow). Different locations of attack excite a different series of partials.

"Harmonics" are partials that are isolated. That is, a harmonic is merely a way of forcing a node or null point in the string to isolate one of the partials; to cause the string to vibrate primarily in one of its partial modes. For example, the harmonic produced by placing the finger lightly on the string at the 12th fret forces the string to vibrate at its first partial — the string vibrating in two equal segments or halves — since the 12th fret is half the distance between the nut and the bridge. On a 5-string banjo, the first string is tuned to fourth octave D at 293.66Hz; the harmonic played at the 12th fret produces a note which is one octave above, the fifth octave D at 587.32Hz (more properly known as D587.32).

LATERAL VS LONGITUDINAL VIBRATIONS

Strings produce energy both laterally and longitudinally. Lateral vibrations are those motions that go side to side (Fig. 2-6), parallel to the length of the string; longitudinal vibrations run the length of the string from the peghead to the bridge. Surprising as it may seem, the longitudinal vibrations are far stronger than the lateral ones. An acoustic guitar with a fixed bridge (no tailpiece) is driven almost entirely by longitudinal vibrations — waves of energy shooting up and down the length of the string, torquing the bridge back and forth. On an acoustic guitar, little or no power is produced by the lateral vibrations, those generated by the lateral direction in which the string is picked.

Longitudinal vibrations (Fig. 2-7) occur in two forms: those that run back and forth *along* the string, and energy that is driven directly *through* the string in a perfectly straight line, as if you stretched an elastic band and released one end. Both modes are important, and a further discussion of the difference and contribution of each goes beyond the scope of this text.

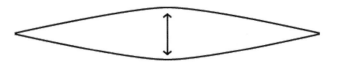

Fig. 2-6. Energy comes from the string in two directions: lateral and longitudinal. Lateral vibrations are those that generate energy perpendicular to the string's axis.

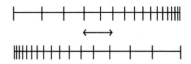

Fig. 2-7. Longitudinal vibrations run the length of the string and are very important to driving most bridge systems.

The power of longitudinal vibrations is the result of a string tuned to pitch, with its tension and elasticity acting as stored energy ready to be released by the string vibrating back and forth. To clarify this, think of a jump rope: each end-holder feels the tug towards the other holder (longitudinal) more than the circular motion (lateral) of the rope. A perfect example of how powerful this energy is can be found in the amplitude of the squeaks made by classical guitar players when their fingers slide back and forth on the wound strings. And, from a standpoint of sheer power, think of the exchange of lateral and longitudinal energy, and how it is released in a bow and arrow. Strings go dead because they lose their elasticity, the energy which is manifest in the longitudinal vibrations. More on this in *Chapter 8, Strings.*

MOVABLE BRIDGES VS FIXED BRIDGES

Thus we enter an important aspect of sound production in stringed musical instruments: the dynamic differences between movable and fixed bridge systems. In fixed bridge systems, those without tailpieces as in acoustic and classical guitars, the soundboard is torqued into a somewhat distorted position by the strings' tension (about 175 pounds pull on a set of medium gauge steel acoustic guitar strings). When the strings are excited, the interaction between soundboard torquing back and forth seeking its state of rest and the strings increasing and decreasing their longitudinal energy, causes the soundboard to act as an efficient air pump which, contained by the body of the guitar, generates areas of compression and rarefaction. If we are close enough before the energy is absorbed by surrounding air, we hear the instrument. Internal bracing is important here to keep the soundboard from bending out of shape, self-destructing, and to control the amount of stiffness of the soundboard. On fixed-bridge instruments, the bridge rocks back and forth on its axis as opposed to moving up and down as might be expected.

On movable bridge instruments, those with tailpieces, we rely mainly on the up and down motion of the bridge since some percentage of the longitudinal vibrations is trapped by the tailpiece. One important aspect in capturing vibrations is the down-pressure at the bridge and more specifically, the angle at which the strings are bent as they cross over the bridge, forcing the bridge down to the soundboard (head). Envision for a moment if the strings went straight back to the tailpiece and just *touched* the bridge; aside from string buzzes, you would hear very little. The greater the angle, the more the strings' energy is driven towards the soundboard, but there are limits and we'll deal more with that in the chapters on bridges and on tailpieces. So, it is on these movable bridge instruments that we take advantage of lateral vibrations as well. In some cases, as in the viol family, the interaction of the bow, strings, bridge, soundboard, soundpost, and backboard is quite a complex matter which also ventures beyond the scope and intent of this text.

Movable bridge instruments don't need braces, since the soundboard is not being torqued or twisted, and it is here that braces called "tonebars" are intended as tools to adjust the stiffness of the soundboard and thus play a role in tuning the instrument's air chamber. And, of course, in the case of the banjo, its thin membrane soundboard (head) is un-braced, since we can adjust its stiffness by tensioning the head material.

THE BANJO AS A TONE PRODUCER

The banjo is complex in nature. Here the longitudinal vibrations rock the bridge slightly (towards and away from the peghead) and force it up and down using the tailpiece as the fulcrum. The greater the *string break angle* (the angle that the strings make when they go over the bridge), the greater the movement of energy to the head. And, as we will see in *Chapter 5, Bridges*, there is an optimum string angle within the logistical problems we have at the banjo bridge: a bridge about 5/8" high resting on a flat soundboard with an anchoring point, the tailpiece, about 2-1/2" away. Energy to the soundboard is also derived from lateral vibrations, driven up and down through the bridge — the result of the head moving up and down as the strings are slacked and tightened — and it is the combination of these two modes which contributes to the banjo's unique sound.

On the banjo, the strings' energy is connected to the soundboard ("head") via a bridge. The soundboard is un-braced, is of consistent thickness across its width and length, and is supported by a rigid rim and tone-ring assembly that damps (absorbs) little or none of the head's vibrations, thus allowing it to sing to its heart's content.

The banjo's bridge is located at a point about one-third of the way across the head, and the exact location of the bridge is critical because the head — much like the strings — also vibrates in modes or partials. The exact point where the head is excited or driven is very important to both the amplitude and the tonal characteristics of the banjo's output. Because of the established fretting scale lengths, and the fact that the fretboard is affixed to the neck, the positioning of the bridge across the head is something we don't have a great deal of control over without major modifications, but can do some experimenting with.

The instrument has a tailpiece that in most cases is moderately adjustable and allows for altering the amount of the strings' down-pressure at the bridge, a very important aspect of amplitude and tonal characteristics. Tailpieces are also manufactured from cast or stamped parts and are available in a variety of lengths, and these are discussed in *Chapter 7, Tailpieces*.

As we will soon discover, the combinations of tone chambers (arched, flathead, drilled, plain, cast, tube, etc.), rims, and attaching hardware present a wide array of tonal characteristics, as well as a very unusual and enjoyable case for the explorative banjo owner and player. Finally, there are open back and resonator back instruments, each with their own complexities.

As far as history tells us, the earliest banjo heads were made of calfskin, which was produced in a wide variety of thicknesses and finishes. The natural skin heads imparted a wonderful warm tone to the instrument, but easily fell victim to changes in humidity and the subsequent plague of rot. Some early head makers developed coated and shellac impregnated heads to fight the moisture, but they proved to rob the instrument of its liveliness. With the age of modern plastics came Mylar, a virtually unbreakable sheeted material from E.I. DuPont, which proved to be a wonderful substitute for skin heads and an even more wonderful tone producer.

Now let's explore each of the components and see what we can do to improve them, one at a time . . .

Pot Assemblies

A banjo's complex metal and wood architecture sets it apart from all other instruments.

The pot assembly — a conventional term given to the body of the banjo — consists of the rim, head, tone chamber or rim rings, and any attaching hardware. The resonator, while an important part of the banjo body, is not considered part of what we refer to as the "pot assembly." The earliest banjos featured wood rims, skin heads, a series of hooks or brackets to tighten the head, shoes or studs to hold the hooks, and a stretcher band onto which the hooks fastened to tighten the head.

As the technology developed, makers sought greater amplitude and clearer tones. The head, one of the most critical tone-producing elements on the banjo, was also the most fickle. Skin heads were prone to rot and tearing and were highly susceptible to changes in the weather, as high humidity brought about moisture absorption that loosened the head and changed its pitch (more on head tuning in *Chapter 9, Tuning the Assembly*). Some head breakage was also due to hidden weaknesses in the natural skin material itself. Head makers, like Ludwig and Jos B. Rogers Jr., developed methods of pressure rolling and chemically treating calfskin heads to make them thinner and smoother, and to close the pores to reduce moisture absorption. By the early 1920s, skin heads were available "pre-stretched" and mounted on a "flesh ring," which greatly improved head alignment and reduced the installation time and the associated assembly headaches.

Wood rims, especially the thinly laminated early versions, provided a poor support — acoustically speaking — for the banjo head. In order for the head to vibrate effectively, and for its vibrations to continue without being damped or absorbed by the rim, the rim needs to have mass (a combination of weight and size). Mass is probably the most essential item that contributes to banjo dynamics. In many lectures I have given, I have expressed that an ideal pot assembly for amplitude (loudness) would be one of cast concrete; a rim which would not damp or absorb any of the head's vibrations (it would also build good shoulder muscles!). While the concrete rim would contribute greatly to amplitude, it would provide little or no *restoring force*. The restoring force is that energy which any component of the instrument gives back to the energy producing member. For example, when a string vibrates and transmits energy to the soundboard or head, the soundboard responds back with similar and temporarily stored energy (created by the string), which helps keep the string in motion. The restoring force is a key element in developing *sustain*.

Obviously, the concrete rim is impractical, and we have come to develop a combination of hardwoods and brass components that deliver an excellent, non-damping, resilient foundation while providing a positive restoring force.

To provide a more rigid support for the head, early makers began to bring metal surfaces in contact with the skin heads. These supports, referred to as "tone rings" and "tone tubes," were seen in a wide range of designs. The basic tone tube was a brass ring placed on top of the wood rim. Brass was chosen instead of steel since it would not rust when the wet head was stretched over the rim, and it was far easier to machine. Some designs were round rod or sheet steel bent and formed over the wood rim, rounded at the corner where the head curves around the upper edge of the rim. These were followed by tubes bent in circles that were either solid or drilled through.

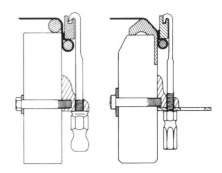

Fig. 3-1. The earliest systems featured "shoes" that were through-bolted to the rim. For resonator banjos, flanges were bolted to the bottom of the shoes.

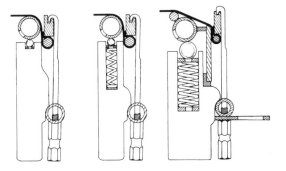

Fig. 3-2. Gibson's ball bearing designs, the basis of George Altermatt's patent shown in Fig. 1-2, evolved to having springs under the ball bearings.

Fig. 3-3. Lloyd Loar's personal TB-5 is a spring-less ball bearing model and the tone tube is drilled (balls are hidden in the rim). The flattened hole in the middle of the lower coordinator rod is where the resonator's thumb screw attaches.

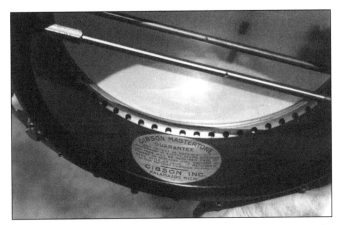

Fig. 3-4. A 1924 Gibson ball bearing model with springs. This model also has a conventional tube and plate flange.

Fig. 3-5. Numerous tone chamber designs were tested and abandoned. This model from Gibson was developed in the mid 1930s and featured large apertures between each bracket.

Fig. 3-6. The banjo shown in Fig. 3-5 had only one coordinator rod, a short rim and a tone chamber comprised of 24 separate segments.

One interesting development, designed by Gibson in 1923, was a "floating tone chamber" (somewhat contradicting the solid rim concept) with, according to the Gibson Catalog, a "non-friction, full floating tone-tube" resting on 20 ball bearings, each which sat on a washer in a recess in the rim (Fig. 3-2). The perforated tone tube was intended to be a secondary tone chamber and was "tuned to pitch" with the hope of providing better upper partials (higher frequencies) to improve the treble qualities of the instrument. In a secondary effort to improve the "floating tone chamber" concept, Gibson announced a spring-loaded tone chamber in 1925 which featured 24 ball bearings, each resting on a heavy spring to provide a highly resilient soundboard. Another purpose of the springs was to counteract the changes in weather and humidity and force the skin head to stay at the same tension. Unfortunately, the changing head tension also resulted in a constantly changing playing action. As the skin slacked, the head would rise. While the "ball bearing tone chambers" provided a bright and lively tone, the change in action, coupled with the difficulty of disassembling and reassembling the instrument with ball bearings rolling everywhere, made it a less popular model. After weighing the attributes of the floating tone chamber for two years, Gibson introduced a one-piece "bell brass" tone chamber.

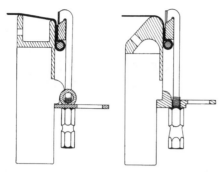

Fig. 3-7. The "flattop" tone chamber (right) increased the head's vibrating area beyond its "archtop" predecessor (left). Note the difference between tube-and-plate and one-piece flange constructions.

Fig. 3-8. Geoff Stelling went against the popular belief that tone chambers had to be hollow and drilled. He designed this highly successful wedge-shaped solid tone-chamber which is drawn to a perfect fit on its wedge-shaped rim.

TONE CHAMBERS: ARCHTOP VS FLATTOP

All of the early manufacturers boasted some form of tone chamber design which made their instruments unique. In late 1927 Gibson announced the "archtop tone chamber" (Fig. 3-7) — a one-piece cast piece whose appearance emulated the two rings of earlier models (the lower outer ring and the raised inner tone tube — see right-hand illustration in Fig. 3-2) — and added the necessary mass for improved amplitude. The design maintained its status for 11 years, and in 1938 Gibson introduced its cast "flattop tone chamber," a design with similar mass to that of the "double bearing" arch-top model, but with an 11" diameter vibrating surface (30.25 sq inches) rather than the 9-1/2" diameter active surface (22.56 sq inches) of its archtop predecessor. While the larger surface area of the flattop tone chamber was almost 50% greater than that of the archtop model, the rim's inside diameter, and unchanged rim-to-resonator aperture (see "Air chamber tuned to pitch," *Chapter 9, Tuning the Assembly*), prevented the instrument from becoming substantially louder. One contribution of the flattop tone chamber was the lower note to which the head could be tuned (see *Chapter 6, Heads*) and the ensuing improvement in lower frequencies (flattops are typically a less treble-sounding instrument). For today's bluegrass musicians, both the flattop and archtop designs are highly respected, while the tonal qualities of the earlier forms of the Paramount, Vega, and Bacon & Day arch-top tone chamber designs continue to be popular with Tenor and Plectrum (4-string) artists.

TONE CHAMBERS: DRILLED VS PLAIN

There is much hypothesis and mystique about the drilled tone chambers (those with holes in them), and numerous studies have been performed on the virtues of drilled vs un-drilled, the number of holes that are necessary, as well as the size and location of the holes. Clearly, Gibson supported a marketing view that the holes provided a tuned air cavity within the tube itself. And, in the words of its catalogs, the tone tube was to support the head and allow it to vibrate on a "highly-sensitive" ring that could "rest free from the rim."

However, the patent for Gibson's ball-bearing tone chamber (G. Altermatt, U.S. Patent No. 1,678,456, July 24, 1928, filed Sept. 23, 1925) speaks about having a sufficiently light tone ring that could move with the head and yet be strong enough to support the crushing force of the head against the balls. Drilling the tube lightened it — one of the goals of his design. In his patent claims, Altermatt does speak of "sound holes" in the tube, but not of "tuning" the chamber.

After doing a great deal of tone chamber experimentation, it is clear that tuning a small space of that nature is 1) a very difficult matter, and 2) highly insignificant to the instrument's overall sound. In light of much controversy, suffice it to say that opening the space to the rest of the air chamber makes a contribution, however insignificant it may be.

One drawback of drilled tone chambers is that drilling disrupts — rather than *improves* — the bell-like quality of the solid tone rings. Specifically, a solid ring has greater acoustical properties than a drilled one. And, to compound the matter, the bell-like qualities quickly vanish when the tone chamber is attached to the wood rim. So, the issue of developing a "bell-like" tone chamber is moot. I have performed exhaustive scientific and empirical tests on drilled and solid tone chambers for both arch-top and flathead instruments. Which is *better* is impossible and ridiculous to say. The un-drilled tone chamber — archtop or flattop — enhances the higher frequencies (see *Chapter 2, How It Works*, "Vibration of Strings"), however minimal they may appear on electronic test equipment, and the audible contribution is virtually imperceptible.

Whether the holes in Gibson's early cast tone chambers were to improve head drying, intentionally reduce the bell-

Fig. 3-9. A center punch or Phillips screwdriver is used through the upper lag screw hole to pry the tone chamber from the rim.

Fig. 3-10. Using a .001″ feeler gauge, squeeze the chamber to the rim and check that the tone chamber contacts the top of the rim.

Fig. 3-11. Inspect the top of the rim. If the instrument has been together for some time, there should be a visible mark where the chamber has taken a set. If not, it's a sign that contact is not adequate.

Fig. 3-12. This excess finish will not affect the contact of a flattop but it is unacceptable for the flush bottom of an archtop tone chamber. (see Fig. 3-7)

like qualities of the brass tone chamber, provide an opening to an additional "tone chamber," or whether they merely resulted from emulating the features of predecessor round tubes may never be factually known. In any case, for RB, Tenor, or Plectrum styles, the drilled tone chambers — 40-holes in the case of the archtop and 20-holes in the case of the flattop — when strung with their respective strings and played in their respective styles, have become the acceptable standard.

TONE CHAMBERS: BELL BRASS VS BRONZE

Brass and bronze come from the same copper base. Brass consists of copper and zinc and is generally softer and less resilient than bronze, which contains copper and tin. As mentioned previously, the idea of having a tone chamber with "bell-like" qualities is somewhat overstated since clamping the tone chamber to a wood rim damps all of its bell-like properties. More important is having a tone chamber which is highly resilient. A steel tone chamber, while expensive to manufacture, would be a perfect substitute for the easily cast and machined brass chambers. The tone chamber must be

dense, stiff, and heavy enough to 1) provide a solid, rigid base for the head, 2) provide a restoring force to the head's vibrations, and 3) not absorb or damp any vibrations.

Improvements You Can Make

1. Tone Chamber Upper Contact. One of the most important contributors to good sound for a banjo is the fit of the tone chamber to the rim. The tone chamber must fit *flush to the top of the rim* before the outer lip of the tone chamber contacts its resting point on the rim. To test the upper fit, disassemble the entire instrument. If the tone chamber falls off during disassembly, you have discovered another problem (see #2 below). Ideally, you would have had to use a small screwdriver in the upper coordinator rod hole to begin to pry the rim and tone chamber loose (Fig. 3-9). Then, using a flat stiff-bladed paint scraper (not a screwdriver, as it will dent the rim or mar the tone chamber), pry the rest of the tone chamber free of the rim. Slip a .001" feeler gauge or a piece of aluminum foil between the tone chamber and the upper part of the rim (Fig. 3-10). Squeeze the tone chamber back in place. While

Fig. 3-15. Proper fitting of tone chambers to rims must be done on a lathe. Here, the author is machining a rim on a custom-made lathe.

Fig. 3-16. Tone chambers should fit the rim so that they have to be squeezed in place *before* the finish is applied to the rim.

squeezing the tone chamber to the rim, you should *not* be able to draw out the feeler gauge. Try it elsewhere on the rim. If it slips free, the tone chamber is riding high on something and not fully contacting the upper edge of the rim, and you must make that correction before reassembly.

If the instrument has been together for some time (10 years or more), you should be able to see a shiny mark on the rim where the ring, finish, and rim have taken a set to each other, indicating good contact. That mark should run all the way around the rim indicating that the tone chamber is making 360° of contact with the rim.

2. Tone Chamber Circumferential Contact. The tone chamber should fit tightly enough to the outer surface of the rim so that you have to squeeze the two parts together with reasonable pressure. If the tone chamber can just slide on and off, the rim must be enlarged for a perfect fit. While the process is difficult to accomplish without a large wood lathe, you can build up several thin beads of epoxy, sanding and fitting between layers until you arrive at the proper fit. Tape off the finished part of the rim so that the epoxy finds its way only to the outer facia of the rim. Do not be concerned if you do not get epoxy all the way down to the lip where the lower portion of the tone chamber contacts the rim (but you must have at least 75% up-and-down coverage for good contact). Regular "5-Minute" epoxy can be used for this process, spreading a thin bead carefully in place with a single edge razor. Apply one coat at a time and allow it to cure fully between coats. For best results, the epoxy should be machined away with the help of a lathe (Fig. 3-15 and 3-16), but hand sanding will work if you take your time. Sand away any high spots by trial and error fitting. Be careful when sanding near the finished part of the rim so that you do not mar the finish. Continue with subsequent applications until you arrive at a good squeeze fit.

3. Tone Chamber Replacement, Same Style. Changing from one manufacturer to another for the same design may require some machining of the rim for an exact fit. Again, be sure the tone chamber contacts the top surface of the rim before the outer lip reaches its stop, and check that the tone chamber fits snugly to the outside face of the rim.

4. Tone Chamber Design Change. Whether you seek the bright treble qualities of the archtop (attributable mainly to the smaller active 9-1/2" diameter head size) or the richer qualities of the flattop (active 11" diameter head size), if you change the tone chamber design, you will have to change or machine the rim. If you seek to change from archtop to flattop, your rim can be machined down approximately 7/32" (this should be check-fitted). However, going from flattop to archtop requires building up the rim approximately 7/32" (which can be done by a competent banjo repair person). Do not attempt to make these changes without access to a lathe capable of chucking and swinging the 11" rim. (Using a standard chuck-less wood lathe will require screwing the rim to the face plate, and this is undesirable.)

RIMS

One very important part of the banjo's coupled system is the rim. Historically, these rims have been produced in a variety of materials, laminations, and constructions. These include: metal-covered single-laminate, three-ply, multi-ply, pie-shaped sections (ala Stelling, see Fig. 3-8), and even Harmony's molded plastic rims.

The wood rims we have come to favor today are made of maple, a comparatively dense wood whose weight averages 40 pounds per cubic foot. I mentioned the weight for two reasons: 1) to reference maple as compared to other woods used in musical instruments (from spruce at 25 pounds per cubic foot to ebony at 70 pounds per cubic foot), and 2) to

Fig. 3-17. There are several combinations of rim ingredients including construction and species of wood. This rim was constructed of steamed and bent Brazilian Rosewood. The sound from the resulting banjo was incredible (and so was the price tag!).

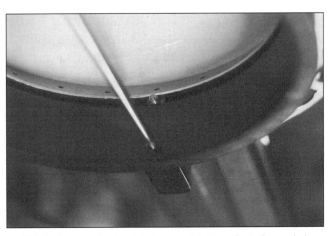

Fig. 3-18. The flattop tone chamber of this foreign made banjo was floating far enough above the rim that the upper lag nut had to be tightened *under* the chamber!

Fig. 3-19. The fit problem for the banjo in Fig. 3-18 was remedied by machining a notch into the rim, gluing in a 1/4" strip of maple, and carefully refitting the tone chamber. The repair resulted in a substantial improvement in tone and dynamics.

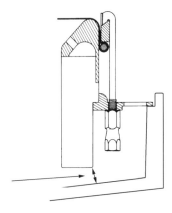

Fig. 3-20. The effective opening or "aperture" (the equivalent of the guitar's soundhole and mandolin's "f" hole) is the space between the bottom of the rim and the inside face of the resonator.

suggest that the mass (again, weight and size) of the rim is important when considering how all the elements work together. For example, because of the design of the Gibson one-piece flange (described further in this section), the rim is cut to 10-5/8" diameter at the lower section and weighs 1 lb, 3 oz, compared to 1 lb, 6 oz for the rim which accompanies the tube-and-plate version (11" at its lower section). Further, the rim used for an archtop tone chamber is heavier than a rim for a flattop tone chamber because of the extra wood needed at the upper edge. Thus, we quickly see that one must consider the contribution of the whole and not just one of its parts. To argue the virtues of tube-and-plate over one-piece flange requires a discussion beyond just the metal components.

Speaking of mass and density, I have made rims of 3-ply rosewood (Fig. 3-17) and of maple-rosewood-maple combinations with excellent results. If you are interested in building a replacement rim for your banjo, I describe several versions in my book *Constructing a Bluegrass Banjo*

(Hal Leonard Corporation, Milwaukee, WI), available at most music stores.

Some early Gibson rims look like 5-ply constructions, but on close inspection the second and fourth laminates are thinner than the rest. These were rims whose laminates were not as successfully glued as others, and in an attempt to save them, the glue seams were re-worked. A cut was made into the laminate line and thin strips of maple were inserted to clean up the joint. These rims are basically 3-ply inside and are totally acceptable as long as the seams have not delaminated.

Improvements You Can Make

1. Structure. If you have a multi-laminated rim, one that looks like plywood from the bottom, you will more than likely notice a positive improvement by replacing that rim with a 3-ply maple rim. Most multi-ply rims do not boast the density and resilience of their 3-ply maple counterparts. The new rim will have to be machined to fit your tone chamber and flange and then stained and finished. (See "Improvements You Can Make" in this chapter under the section on "Tone Chambers: Bell Brass vs Bronze.")

2. Tone Chamber Fit. The rim must fit snugly to the tone chamber and contact the tone chamber at the rim's upper surface before contacting the tone chamber at its outer lip. The rim can be built up to correct for any sloppiness. (See "Improvements You Can Make" in this chapter under the section on "Tone Chambers: Bell Brass vs Bronze.")

3. Affective Aperture. The "affective aperture" is the opening between the rim and the inside of the resonator and is one of the most critical elements for proper tuning of the air chamber (Fig. 3-20). This measurement is often overlooked in banjo construction, and in some cases the rim will have to be turned down to reduce the depth of the rim. (It is more typical that we find it necessary to turn the rim down to shorten it, rather than building it up.) This adjustment and alternatives to shortening the rim are fully discussed in *Chapter 9, Tuning the Assembly.*

STRETCHER BAND

The stretcher band is the ring to which the hooks are attached — it slips over the head to secure it in place. There are two basic types of stretcher bands: notched and grooved. The notched bands have a specific space for each hook to fit into, and the top of the band is flat and smooth between the hooks. The grooved bands have a groove running around the entire top of the band and the hook can fit anywhere. Grooved bands are usually accompanied by "flat" hooks, notched bands with round hooks.

Since both types of bands and their associated hooks weigh about the same, their contribution to the acoustical properties of the banjo is basically equal.

Improvements You Can Make

1. Grooved vs Notched. Both grooved and notched stretcher bands were popular on various banjo models and both contribute equally to the instrument's sound. To achieve proper hook-to-band fit, flat hooks should be used only with grooved bands, and round hooks should be used only with notched bands.

2. Stretcher Band to Neck Fit. Ideally, the neck and the end of the fretboard should contact the stretcher band, rather than having a space there. This adds stiffness to the entire assembly. A tight fit also prevents the neck from damping or absorbing any vibrations. Further, any minimal longitudinal vibrations are more efficiently transferred back to the pot assembly with a proper neck-heel fit, which includes the end of the fretboard contacting the stretcher band. See "#2, Neck to Stretcher Band Fit" under "Improvements You Can Make," *Chapter 2, Necks.*

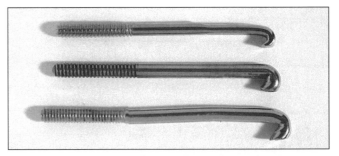

Fig. 3-21. Top to bottom: "Flat" hook with 8x32 thread, round hook with 8x26 thread, round hook with 8x32 thread. (Shown actual size.)

SHOES AND HOOKS

On many early models, the entire rim assembly was held together by shoes, small cast or machined parts that were held in place with screws through the rim. The hooks were attached from the stretcher band through the shoes, and the nuts were tightened to draw the head to its proper tension. On some models, singular stamped plates were positioned under each shoe to provide a flange-like array which covered the opening in the resonator. By the early 1910s full circular flanges, both stamped and cast, were popular.

Improvements You Can Make

1. Attaching Hardware. On instruments with shoes, be sure that nuts holding the shoes to the rim are very snugly tightened. On those instruments with hex nuts to hold the shoes, use a socket wrench, not an open-end or crescent wrench (to prevent slipping and marring the inside of the rim).

2. Hooks and Nuts. Hooks were made with two threads. Most early instruments, including Gibson models, had an unusual 8x26 (#8 screw, 26 threads to the inch) thread. Many hooks were also made with a standard 8x32 thread. The coarser thread was a popular machine screw size at the turn of the century and permitted faster tuning of the skin heads (less turns needed), whereas the finer 8x32 threads provide greater mechanical advantage for smoother and easier tensioning. Most importantly, if you have both available to you, ensure that the nuts can be hand tightened first so that you do not accidentally cross-thread with the wrong nut.

FLANGES AND ATTACHING HARDWARE

The flange is that supporting element which affixes the brackets, holds the resonator to the rim, and covers the opening of the resonator. In some cases, such as the Gibson tube-and-plate and one-piece flanges, the flange assembly replaced the earlier bolt-on shoes. Gibson's first system was a tube which was drilled to accept the hooks and fitted against a lip in the rim. Aside from replacing the 24 shoes and related bolts and washers, the tube had greater structural integrity, was more efficient to assemble, and did not call for drilling 24 holes into the wood rim. In 1925, with

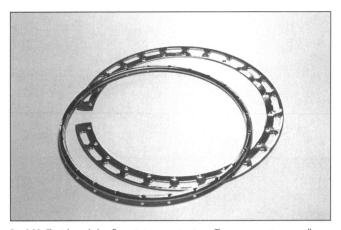

Fig. 3-22. The tube and plate flange is two separate pieces. These components are usually made from brass.

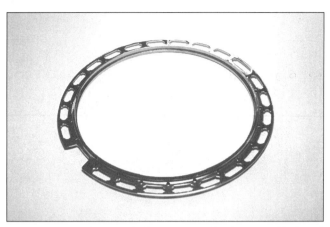

Fig. 3-23. The one-piece flange is made of zamac ("pot metal"), which casts and finishes well but is rather brittle. Exercise care removing them from your banjo.

the announcement of its line of full resonator banjos, and following developments already in place from Paramount, Bacon & Day, and others, Gibson added a stamped plate below the tube, held in place by the same nuts used to tighten the hooks. In 1929 Gibson developed a one-piece cast flange that emulated the tube and plate design, but was a simplified single-element zamac ("pot metal") casting.

As mentioned previously, the tube-and-plate flanges feature a heavier rim while the one-piece flanges, although heavier themselves because they were cast parts, feature a lighter rim. (The cut of rims was different due to the difference in flange-to-rim assembly requirements.) As with our other discussions on coupled systems, the combination of one-piece flange and lighter rim provided different tonal qualities than the tube-and-plate and heavier rim.

Most importantly, due to the differences in design of the one-piece flange and tube-and-plate systems, and more specifically, where the flange is seated on the waist of the respective rims relative to the bottom of the rim, the one-piece flange causes the entire pot assembly to sit lower in the resonator than on tube-and-plate models. This lower positioning of the rim closes the effective aperture (the space between the bottom of the rim and the inside face of the resonator) and substantially lowers the resonant frequency (pitch) of the air chamber, and it is this different positioning of the pot assembly that causes an additional difference in tonal properties between these two systems. We'll study more about this in *Chapter 9, Tuning the Assembly*.

Over the years, manufacturers have developed various methods of attaching the resonator to the pot assembly. At the introduction of Gibson's Mastertone line, four angle brackets were screwed into the rim, which aligned with four studs screwed into the inner wall of the resonator, and the assembly was held together with four thumb screws. In the mid '50s this was reduced to three brackets, studs, and

screws, and by 1980, Gibson developed a stamped plate which was held onto the flange assembly by the hooks and nuts. The earlier angle brackets rested on the resonator's inner lip and held the flange above it, as did the stamped plates of the 1980s. The mid '50s angle brackets were short and allowed the flange to rest on the resonator's lip. As we will learn in *Chapter 9, Tuning the Assembly*, these brackets can be important tools for positioning the pot assembly relative to the resonator for tuning the air chamber.

Improvements You Can Make

1. Flange Style Changes. There isn't really much you can do here, and changing from one design to another is impractical because of the design differences in the wood rims. Bear in mind that if you want to change from tube-and-plate to one-piece flange, both the rim and the neck heel cut are different. If you choose to make this change, you will need to change both the rim and the flange.

2. Tube-and-Plate Fit. This is acceptable if the tube fits loosely onto the rim's lip. When the hooks are tightened, the tube will be pulled in place. The plate should be flat and have no bends or kinks in it, so that solid contact will be made between the tube and the plate when the nuts are tightened.

3. One-Piece Flange Fit. The one piece flange does not have the rounded, self-fitting qualities of the tube on the tube-and-plate design, and it should, therefore, be well fitted to the rim so that it requires a squeeze fit into place at its contact point. Since this is a finished cosmetic surface, it cannot be as easily refitted as a tone chamber can if a fit problem occurs (See "Improvements You Can Make," #1 and #2 in this chapter under "Tone Chambers: Bell Brass vs Bronze.") If the flange lip needs to be refitted, it is best to cut into the rim, glue in a 1/4" piece of maple, and re-machine. This work should be left to a competent repair person. Of course, the rim will need to be refinished.

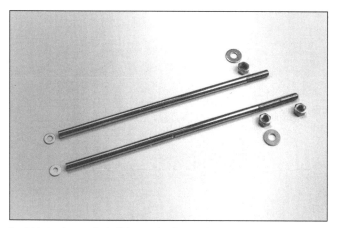

Fig. 3-24. Coordinator rods should have washers between the rods and the rim at the lag-screw end, and between the nuts and the rim at the tailpiece end.

Fig. 3-25. It is important to use tools that fit when adjusting coordinator rods. A small Philips screwdriver or center punch works well for the hole in the coordinator rods.

COORDINATOR RODS AND DOWEL STICKS

Two main methods have been used to hold necks to rims: dowel sticks and metal rods. The dowel stick is a wood connection that is typically glued into the neck. In most cases, the action cannot be easily adjusted with a dowel stick. However, some early manufacturers provided for adjustment of the neck angle by turning a screw at the tailpiece end of the dowel stick (inside the banjo's air chamber). Metal rods have been employed by several manufacturers, and Gibson developed a scheme of two "coordinator" rods that allowed for adjustment of the neck angle.

Improvements You Can Make

1. Dowel Stick Adjustments. Some dowel-stick banjos have neck-pitch adjusting mechanisms where the dowel stick attaches to the tailpiece edge of the rim. These adjustments are pretty straightforward. However, changing the neck angle with a solid dowel-stick assembly should be left to the luthier, as proper adjustment may call for removal and realignment of the stick or resetting of the position of the end screw. Minor adjustments can sometimes be made by filling in the hole for the end screw (where the dowel stick attaches the tailpiece) and relocating the hole up or down, depending on whether you wish to raise or lower the action of the neck.

2. Coordinator Rod Adjustments. Coordinator rods should be tightened securely to the neck bolts before any of the other nuts are tightened. Be sure to have washers between the coordinator rods and the inside of the rim. Use a nail or small punch through the holes in the middle of the coordinator rods — never user pliers! Once the neck is secure, snug up the nut on the upper rod and snug up the two nuts on the lower rod. Bring the strings up to pitch.

NOTES
1. *Before making any adjustments, read* Chapter 5, Bridges *to determine the correct bridge height.*

2. *In each of the following adjustments, the coordinator rods should remain tightly connected to the neck and rim.*

To lower the action: (to decrease the distance between the last fret nearest the head and any string) first try loosening the *inside lower nut* and tightening the *outside lower nut*. To do this, place a nail or small punch in the hole in the coordinator rod. Using an open-end wrench (not pliers) of the proper size, loosen the large inside nut on the lower coordinator rod, tighten the outside nut one-quarter turn, and retighten the inside nut. Check the string action — the ideal space between the 3rd string and the 12th fret should be 3/32" (2mm).

Repeat the adjustment if better action is required. If the desired distance is not obtained after one and a half turns of the lower outside nut (after it was first hand tightened), try to tighten the upper inside nut. No more than one full turn should be placed on this nut. If further adjustment is required, you will have to shim or recut the neck heel. For this procedure, refer to the section entitled "#3) Action" in the section "Improvements You Can Make," in *Chapter 4, Necks.*

To raise the action: (to increase the distance between the last fret nearest the head and any string) first try loosening the *outside lower nut* and tightening the *inside lower nut*. To do this, place a nail or small punch in the hole in the coordinator rod. Using an open-end wrench (not pliers) of the proper size, loosen the large outside nut on the lower coordinator rod, tighten the inside nut one-quarter turn, and retighten the outside nut. Check the string action — the ideal distance between the 3rd string and the 12th fret should be 3/32" (2mm).

NOTE
With the neck under string tension, you may find that you do not have to actually "tighten" the inside nut. String tension alone may pull the nut away from the rim as the outside nut is loosened.

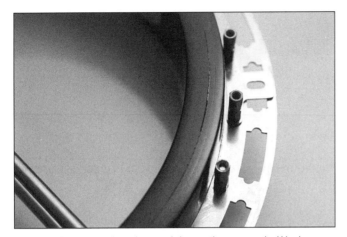
Fig. 3-26. Unfortunately, cracks in glue joints do happen. The instrument should be disassembled and reglued before the seam opens further.

Repeat the adjustment if higher action is required. If the desired distance is not obtained after one-and-a-half turns of the lower inside nut (after it was first hand tightened), then try to loosen the upper inside nut, but not to the point where it goes slack. If further adjustment is required beyond what you can do with the coordinator rods, you will have to shim or recut the neck heel. For this procedure, refer to the section entitled "#3 Action" under "Improvements You Can Make," in *Chapter 4, Necks.*

Maintenance Tips

1. Metal Parts. Nickel and gold parts tend to dull over time (chrome is a bit more durable, but it is not typically used in banjo parts). Once a year, it is a good idea to disassemble the instrument and clean all metal parts with a delicate jewelry-type metal polish.

CAUTION

Gold parts may be coated with a clear lacquer which does not clean easily, and could "blush" if a strong cleaner is used. Real gold cleans quickly and easily. Never use abrasive cleaners, as repeated use can remove gold. Try your cleaning chemicals on a less visible area first.

NOTE

In the plating process, gold plating is done over nickel plating, and this is why we often see gold wearing away and leaving a nickel surface in its place.

2. Loose Parts. The banjo should be checked for loose nuts, including those on the tailpiece, coordinator rods, bracket hooks, and armrest. It is not typical to experience changes in rim-to-tone chamber fit, but checking it once every two years is prudent.

3. Cracks and "Checks." Failures in metal parts rarely occur on banjo pot assemblies. However, I have seen numerous cracked tailpieces which have broken at their bent and formed corners. This is another reason I suggest using heavy tailpieces. Older brass does fatigue and little or nothing can be done to repair or strengthen these parts to make them usable.

Occasionally, some of the older two-piece armrests will come apart at their soldered joints. These can be resoldered, but it typically causes discoloration that will require replating. I have seen a few of these that have been very cleanly riveted.

A seam crack in a rim will destroy its acoustical properties. Rims do de-laminate, and the opened seam should be repaired as soon as possible. The bottom of the rim can be easily inspected by removing the resonator. Seam cracks show up easily because the finish will also crack.

"Checks" are hairline cracks in the grain of the wood. Checking sometimes occurs in ebony fretboards if the banjo has been left in a very dry environment for a prolonged period. Checks rarely occur in neck, resonator, or rim wood or other finished areas. Inspect the end of the neck for checking during periodic tear-downs (once every two years).

Necks

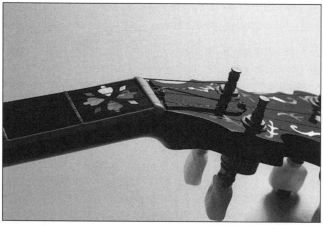

While the neck is the musician's control tower, it plays a secret yet vital role in the instrument's acoustical system.

BACKGROUND OF THE NECK

The neck provides the instrument with a means for adjusting the strings to pitch and, of course, for playing the instrument by accessing the strings to press them against the frets.

The most popular banjos were four-string models in both plectrum (26" string scale, 22 frets) and tenor (21" string scale, 18 frets, and 23" scale with 19 frets). Although the standard bluegrass "RB" banjo has a 26" scale with 22 frets, five-string, or "regular banjos," were available from most manufacturers in a wide variety of string scales from short 15 fret models to Vega's 30" string scale, 24-fret "Pete Seeger" model.

To simplify the marketing process, string scales were typically rounded to the nearest 1/4". For example, Gibson's popular 23" tenor scale was actually 22-5/8".

Most cataloged model changes were basically a neck change on a standard pot assembly, and numerous banjo models were promoted for artists who specialized in ukulele, guitar, and mandolin fingerings and styles, and thus could provide their artistry with the banjo's voicing.

Fretboards were typically made of rosewood or ebony, both of which provided good string-to-fretboard wear resistance, and fretwire was available in a wide array of sizes and metals.

As in other things we have learned relative to *coupled systems* in this text, the neck wood played an important contribution to the instrument's overall sound. Mahogany or walnut instruments were typically not as bright as their maple, rosewood (ala Paramount), or laminated counterparts. And, heavy tuning machines (especially those fitted with large mother-of-pearl knobs) at the peghead seemed to make a valuable contribution to sustain by preventing vibrations from "wicking" off the end of the neck.

Some performers talk of hearing the difference between holding the neck in the hand (thus damping or absorbing vibrations) versus using the thumb on the back of the neck in the classical tradition. In either case, a solid neck, made of a high-density wood and well fitted to the pot assembly, appears to provide the best solution for a bright and powerful banjo sound.

The stiffness, weight, grain (direction), and density of the neck wood plays a major role in the overall tonal properties of the instrument. Choice of wood is something you can select at the outset but probably will not wish to modify with your existing instrument. Early Paramount instruments featured rosewood necks, and rosewood is a wonderful (and very expensive) material to use. It transmits sound so well that it is used for various rhythm instruments of South America such as "claves," and the tone producing bars of some xylophones and marimbas. Maple is equally wonderful, but curly maple can be tricky as the wavy grain (what you see as the "curl") offers a less rigid material than its straight grained counterpart. Mahogany is incredibly stabile due to the overlapping growth rings and internal structure of the wood, but it is not a great tone producer. Walnut, while not as stabile as mahogany, has similar acoustical properties. To give you a better idea of the relationship of the density and weight of these woods, this chart may be helpful:

> Brazilian rosewood: 53-63 pounds per cubic foot
> Sugar maple: 40 pounds per cubic foot
> Red maple: 35-37 pounds per cubic foot
> Black walnut: 36-37 pounds per cubic foot
> Honduras mahogany: 34-39 pounds per cubic foot

Typically, the higher the density and mass (weight and size taken as a whole), the better the acoustical properties.

NOTE
"Curly" maple is not a species, but instead, a phenomenon in wood growth. Curl happens in many species of woods and is most common to deciduous trees. "Curly," "flamed," "fiddle-back," and "tiger" maple are all common terms given to the same phenomenon.

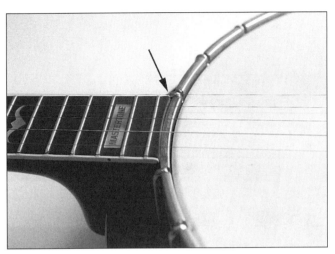

Fig. 4-1. This 1980 RB-250 had a space between the end of the neck and the stretcher band. Inserting a shim made a noticeable difference in sustain and clarity.

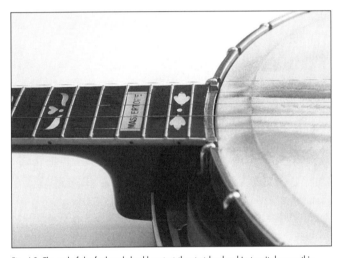

Fig. 4-2. The end of the fretboard should contact the stretcher band just as it does on this 1926 RB-3.

Fig. 4-3. If the desirable change in action cannot be made with *moderate* coordinator rod adjustment, a plastic shim between the neck and rim (around the upper or lower lag screw) can make the difference.

The neck fit, angle, height, and contact to the stretcher band are all very important to the acoustical integrity of the instrument, and these topics are discussed in the following section on "Improvements You Can Make."

Many of the earlier instruments featured laminated necks boasting numerous species of woods, both dyed and natural. The laminated necks provided excellent stability from warpage and added a great deal of desired stiffness to the neck structure.

Improvements You Can Make

1. Neck to Rim Fit. The neck should fit flush and securely to the rim assembly. The end of the fretboard should firmly contact the stretcher band (see #2, below). Coordinator rods or dowel sticks should draw the neck tightly to the rim.

NOTE

The neck lag screws are machine screws at one end and wood screws at the other that go about 1-1/2" into the neck wood's end-grain. They can be pulled out of the wood if excessive tightening force is placed on the coordinator rods. See the "Coordinator Rod Adjustment" section in Chapter 3, Pot Assemblies, for the correct amount of tightening pressure.

2. Neck to Stretcher Band Fit. Since one end of the strings is connected to the peghead, the neck plays a role in delivering some of the strings' energy to the pot assembly. For optimum transmission of the longitudinal vibrations, the end of the fretboard should contact the stretcher band (Figs. 4-1 and 4-2). Many banjo heels are cut so that there is a gap between the fretboard and the stretcher band, and this should be remedied.

This is a simple matter and it can be corrected with a shim of thin (black or clear) plastic, brass, or aluminum (Fig. 4-3). Cut a piece of the selected material to fit the required height and width, slacken the strings, loosen the coordinator rods, insert the shim, and retighten. The shim should be thick enough so that it can be forced just a short distance into the space while the instrument is assembled, but cannot be fully put in place until the instrument is disassembled. Under no circumstances should the shim be thicker than a force fit. When the coordinator rods are retightened, they should snug the shim in place and not put undue or uneven stress on the stretcher band or neck heel.

The added contact will also provide greater stability and lessen the chance of pitch changes when the neck is pushed forward. Further, there will be better structure to support the neck when the instrument is carried or lifted from the case.

3. Action. Should the neck need to be realigned to change the action, the adjustment can be made by a) adjusting the coordinator rods, b) recutting the heel of the neck, or c) shimming the neck. Coordinator rod adjustment is explained in *Chapter 3, Pot Assemblies*. Recutting or reshap-

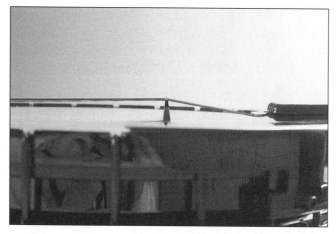

Fig. 4-4. String angle determines how much energy is driven down to the head. The angle is measured at the bridge and is the result of correct tailpiece height, bridge height, neck height, and neck angle.

Fig. 4-5. If the neck sits too high, the strings are raised and the correct string angle cannot be achieved.

Fig. 4-6. This banjo had plenty of space between the bottom of the neck and the notch in the resonator, allowing the neck to be lowered without further adjustment to the resonator.

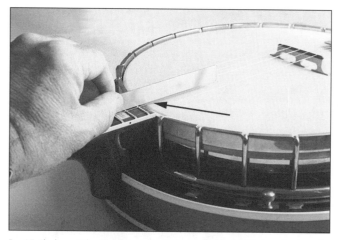

Fig. 4-7. The line or "plane" of the neck should be no more than 3/32" above the plane of the soundboard (head) where the two meet.

ing should be carried out by a competent instrument craftsman, and must be crafted so that 1) the curved faces of the neck heel mate perfectly to the surfaces of the rim, 2) the lateral attitude of the cut is such that there is a straight line from the center of the peghead, through the center of the last fret at the stretcher band, to the center of the tailpiece, 3) there is a square rotational attitude of the neck so that the fretboard and head are on identical planes, 4) the proper neck angle is achieved to obtain the correct string angle over the bridge and string height over the head, and 5) to obtain the proper fretboard-to-head alignment (height). To change the neck angle, shimming is perfectly acceptable and easily accomplished, but only plastic, brass, aluminum, or metal should be used as shims, never paper.

The ideal playing action is a 3/32" (2mm) space between the 1st string and the top of the twelfth fret, and about 5/64" (2.5mm) between the 4th string and the twelfth fret. Note that proper action calls for more space under the 4th string and less space under the 1st string, since the heavier

4th string vibrates in larger orbits and is more prone to cause unwanted buzzes if the action is too low.

The ideal neck angle is 3° to the soundboard (head) plane (Fig. 4-4). With a 5/8" bridge, this will yield a 15° string angle over the bridge. With a 9/16" bridge, it will yield a 14° string angle. For additional information on string angle, see "#1, Down Pressure" in *Chapter 7, Tailpieces*.

4. Neck Height. In addition to changing the neck angle, it may become necessary to alter the neck height to achieve the correct playing action at the 12th fret and the correct string angle at the bridge. Note that while the neck angle and neck height are interrelated, they are still separate adjustments. Further, if the desired action has been achieved but the string angle at the bridge is still too shallow, then the neck may have to be moved down, requiring several changes including, but not limited to 1) resetting the position of the lag screws in the neck heel, 2) recutting the neck heel, and 3) elongating the neck notch in the resonator. These adjustments should be left to

Fig. 4-8. To lower the neck, the lag screws need to be repositioned. Lags are easily and safely removed by locking two 10x32 nuts to each other and then turning the lags out with a socket driver.

Fig. 4-9. Two maple dowels were turned to the right size and glued into the drilled-out lag screw holes.

a competent luthier. Be cautioned that the bottom lag screws on early Gibson banjos (1924 – 1940) are L-shaped, embedded into the neck heel, and cannot be unscrewed. The use of L-shaped lag screws can be determined by the presence of a wood filler strip between the lag screw and the heel cap.

The necks on some brands of banjos are fitted rather high (Fig. 4-5), such that the plane of the fretboard is much higher than the plane of the soundboard (head). The higher the neck is fitted, the more difficult it is to achieve the proper string angle over the bridge. The neck should be reset so that the plane of the fretboard — not the *angle* of the fretboard — is no more than 3/32" above the plane of the soundboard (head) where the two meet (Fig. 4-7). For example, you should be able to place one straightedge on the frets and another one on the soundboard plane. Where the rulers intersect over the stretcher band, the distance should not exceed 3/32" (2mm) (Fig. 4-11).

5. Frets. Heavy playing and especially a heavy left hand will cause fret wire to wear under the strings. This lowered spot eventually leads to unwanted noise and buzzes as the frets become un-level with each other. Fretwire is easily changed; however, the process calls for special expertise and tools, and the work should be done by a competent instrument repair person.

6. Machines. Geared machines should be checked from time to time for loose knobs, which are often the subject of errant buzzes. Most machine knobs have screws at the end which can be tightened and adjusted for drag.

Once a year, place *one drop* of motor oil on the peg shaft, and turn the machine with the strings off so that the oil can work its way down into the housing.

NOTE
Do not use 3-in-One or similar light-grade oil (heavy oil will cling to the gears and not spread onto the surrounding areas).

7. Truss Rod. The truss rod — and almost all banjos made after 1920 have them — is a round steel rod embedded in the neck, with one end fixed to the heel end of the neck and an adjustment nut fitted at the peghead end. Under normal conditions, the strings' tension wants to bend the neck to a *hollow* (where the action of the strings is higher in the center of the fretboard than at either end). The rod is designed to counteract the force of the string tension and keep the neck straight.

By carefully tightening the nut (using a socket wrench), the neck will be forced to *bow* (raising the center of the fretboard towards the strings), and loosening the nut will cause it to bend into a *hollow* (some luthiers call it a *warp*). An ideal way to check the straightness of the neck is to press down on any string at both the nut end and heel end of the fretboard. The ideal fretboard will have just a slight space (.015" is recommended) between the string and the middlemost fret.

NOTE
If the string contacts a middle fret before the string touches the frets on either end of the fretboard, it will indicate a bow in the neck which is sure to be the cause of buzzes and unwanted rattles.

To adjust the rod, it is wise to help the neck into a bow by applying slight bending pressure. The instrument should be strung and up to pitch while the adjustment is being made. Lay the banjo on a table (with protection under the resonator), and place a padded object under the *middle* of the neck (a few books with a towel between the neck and books will do), allowing the peghead end of the neck to protrude from the end of the table. Now, by applying slight downward pressure on the peghead, the neck will be forced into a bow and the truss rod can be adjusted. Make half turns between testing the action. If the neck does not want to bow, or if you feel restriction on the nut, consult a competent instrument repair person before going any further.

Fig. 4-10. The neck heel was recut and the lags were relocated to a *higher* position (thus lowering the neck). Recesses around the lag screw holes allow flush contact between neck and rim.

Fig. 4-11. The change lowered the neck so that it was flush to the plane of the head and added 3° to the string angle at the bridge. (Compare the neck height to the same instrument in Fig. 4-5.)

NOTE

Use a socket wrench that fits the nut perfectly. You should not have to apply great force to make the correction.

Another important property of the truss rod, in addition to altering the neck's plane, is that it also affects the stiffness of the neck wood. Although this contribution of the truss rod to brightness and tambre is minimal, it does have an affect. On the other hand, a loose truss rod will cause unwanted buzzes and rattles.

8. Lag Screws. Just a word of caution here: As previously mentioned, the pre-1940s Gibson banjos have an L-shaped lower lag screw embedded in the neck heel under the heel cap. It cannot be unscrewed. (The upper one is threaded into the neck.) Relative to the scope of this text, there are no adjustments that need to be made to the lag screws unless one breaks.

THE NUT

The nut is a critical element in setting the action above the frets (Fig. 4-12), establishing the distance between the strings, and maintaining the alignment of the strings relative to the fretboard and axis of the neck. There are basically two types of nuts: a conventional nut and a zero-action nut (sometimes called a zero-fret).

The conventional nut, the more desirable of the two, is notched by the manufacturer and is designed so that the strings are set in the nut at the intended height or "action" above the fretboard. This is a science carefully exercised by most manufacturers, and once the nut is set by the manufacturer, it rarely needs adjustment.

The zero-action nut has a fret installed immediately in front of the nut which establishes the correct height of the string above the fretboard and basically facilitates the installation and adjustment of the nut. However, since this system calls for the slot in the nut to be deeper than the height of the fretwire (so that the string can sit on top of the fret and not touch the bottom of the notch in the nut), there is often a chance for string noise at the fret. Zero-action nuts are usually found on less expensive instruments.

Nuts on early banjos were made of bone, with some models featuring pearl, ebony, or — in the early days — ivory. Today, many manufacturers use Mycarta — a synthetic bone-like material from DuPont — or other similar substitutes. The Corean used for making sinks is another excellent material. The nut must be made from a hard dense material so that it does not wear, chip, or damp the vibrations of the strings.

String notches should be cut as V-shaped grooves so that the string rests against side walls of the notch and is not allowed to vibrate in the bottom of the notch. Also, the string groove should be angled halfway between the plane of the fretboard and the plane of the peghead so that the string makes positive contact where it both enters *and* leaves the nut.

Geoff Stelling introduced an interesting idea of intonating the nut — correcting the string length of each string to compensate for gauge and fretting anomalies (Fig. 4-13). To do this, he alters the contact point where each string leaves the nut. While I believe compensations should be made at the bridge (see *Chapter 5, Bridges*), Geoff's development seems to work quite well.

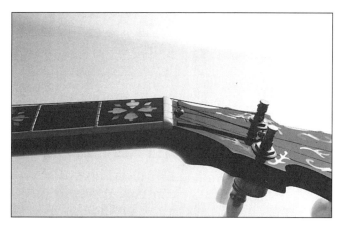

Fig. 4-12. Strings should firmly contact the nut and provide proper playing *action* at the first fret (described further in this section).

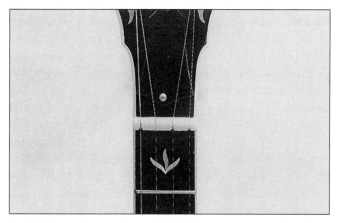

Fig. 4-13. The intonation-corrected nuts on Stelling banjos are designed to correct for tuning anomalies.

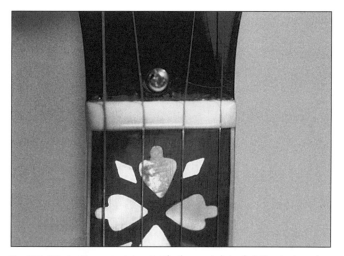

Fig. 4-14. String-to-string spacing is important for the correct playing feel. There is plenty of fretboard width for these strings to be more widely spaced. While each musician has his or her preference, most would prefer a string-to-string distance of no less than 5/16".

Improvements You Can Make

1. Rattles and Buzzes. Noises from the nut can be rather quickly detected by playing each string and pressing a finger on that string on the peghead side of the nut. If the buzz goes away, it is most likely caused by improper string fit at the nut. Carefully examine the nut. If you can move the strings side to side, the notches are either worn or cut too large.

Sometimes it is helpful to touch the suspect string in the string notch with a small screwdriver (pressing it down into the nut slot) while picking the suspect string — this may help to locate the buzz. If you determine that the buzz is caused by the slots being too wide, you may still be able to save the nut, as long as you can lower the slot in the nut if you find that the action is too high. In this case, follow the steps in "Improvements You Can Make," "3) Action," in *Chapter 4, Necks.*

If the slots are too wide and the strings cannot be lowered, then it is necessary to change the nut. Since this procedure may lead to cosmetic work where the finish joins the nut, I would suggest turning the job over to an instrument repairperson. If you want to attempt the work, the nut can be loosened by a) removing the strings, b) using a #11 Xacto blade to score the lacquer where it meets the joints of the nut, peghead and fretboard, c) placing a small wood block against fretboard side of the nut, d) tapping the block gently until the nut comes lose, e) removing it, and f) fashioning a new one to match the original one from either bone, pearl, abalone, or one of the synthetics previously mentioned, and gluing it in place using a small dab of Duco cement.

NOTE
Shape the nut, mark and cut the string slots, and sand the nut smooth while it is off of the instrument. Only final action adjustments should be done while the nut is on the instrument and only after the glue has set.

2. Action at the Nut. If the string action is too high, you can correct it by refiling the notch with a jewelers file that is "V" shaped. Hold the file at an angle that is halfway between that of the peghead and the fretboard. Make straight deliberate passes with the file, blow the dust out of the slot, and check the string action after every two passes with the file. The right action at the nut can be determined by measuring the space between each string and the first fret; the correct space should be .006" (six thousandths of an inch) for the 1st string, ranging to .007" (seven thousandths of an inch) for the 4th string at the first fret.

Do not use a triangular file as it will make too wide a "V" — the cross-section of the file must be "V" or double-"V."

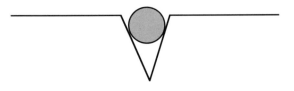

Fig. 4-15. The string notch in the nut should be "V"-shaped so that the string is locked to the walls of the slot. "U"-shaped slots allow strings to slop around and create buzzes.

3. Action That Is Too Low. If the action is too low, you need to change the nut. Follow the steps in the previous paragraph, "1. Rattles and Buzzes" for changing the nut.

5TH-STRING NUT

The 5th-string nut is intended primarily as a guide to hold the string in alignment along the fretboard. It is usually preferred that the fifth fret acts as a zero-nut, allowing the string to contact the fret and not sit in the 5th-string nut's notch. However, if the nut is made of bone, pearl, or some other very dense material and it is secured in place, it is satisfactory if the string rests in the nut without touching the fret.

Improvements You Can Make

Broken 5th-String Nut. Occasionally, the sides of the nut will break from wear and tear. Depending on how the nut is fabricated, you will need to remove the old one and make a new one to take its place. Removal of broken 5th-string nuts can be tricky and may need to be drilled out — a procedure that should be left to a competent repairperson. Bone, pearl, and abalone work well for 5th-string nuts, and in the absence of a small lathe, they can easily be turned to shape by using an electric hand drill and a flat file. Take careful measurements as you proceed. Cut the slot in the top of the nut with a jeweler's saw, or, should that not be available to you, you can create the slot with a jeweler's "V" file. However, if a V-file is used, exercise care to assure that the depth of the cut is just below the height of the fret. Any deeper and the string will be supported too loosely in the widening "V" slot.

5TH-STRING CAPOS

Traditionally, 5th-string capos have been added to assist in adjusting the 5th string to the correct pitch when using a capo to play in other keys. Two types of 5th-string capos exist: a sliding capo that affixes to the side of the neck (a little clumsy if you plan to fret the 5th string with your thumb), and small nails or clips placed into the fretboard to hold the 5th string down at the 7th and 10th frets (preferred).

Improvements You Can Make

1. Installing Sliding 5th-String Capos. These capos are screwed into the side of the neck and will require drilling of two pilot holes before the screws can be installed. Follow the instructions of the manufacturer. Exercise care so that the drill or screwdriver does not slip during installation. Double check your measurements and positioning before drilling the pilot holes.

2. Installing 5th-String Nails. Typically, HO-gauge model railroad spikes are used for 5-string nails. Since these are most likely being driven into ebony or rosewood, you will have to drill small pilot holes first. The first nail usually is positioned at the 7th fret (Fig. 4-16), for using a capo in the A position, and the second one at the 10th fret for playing in B or C. Position the 7th fret nail so that it faces in towards the fretboard, and the 10th fret nail so that it faces to the outside of the neck. In this way, when using the first nail at the 7th fret, the string will be drawn away from the head of the second nail. The nails should be positioned 3/16" behind the fret and installed just low enough so that the string can be easily slipped under it.

Maintenance Tips

1) The neck and strings should be wiped down after each use to remove dirt and natural oils. Use a clean, dry, lintless rag.

2) Ebony and rosewood fretboards should be wiped down occasionally with a light coating of lemon oil furniture polish. Do not saturate the wood. Use the oil only for cleaning and to restore the wood's luster. Wipe off any excess.

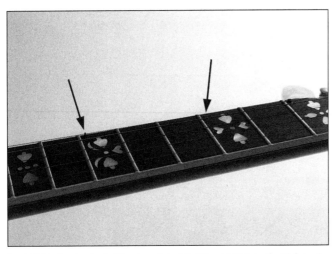

Fig. 4-16. The best location for 5th string nails is at the 7th and 10th frets. The 7th fret nail faces inward and the 10th fret nail faces outward.

3) Banjos which are loosely packed in their cases are prone to neck breakage. Take care that the instrument fits the case properly. If it does not and you determine that the instrument can rattle back and forth in the case, use your cleaning rag over the neck, directly above the neck support in the case, to help hold the instrument in place when the cover is closed.

•

NOTE

The cover must close naturally without force so the neck is not subjected to excessive pressure.

4) Exercise care with vinyl straps. Some vinyl materials will cause a chemical reaction with lacquers and leave blemishes. If you are not sure of the compatibility (the strap manufacturer will usually provide a "safe" statement on the tag), then be sure to fold the strap into the case around the pot assembly so that its vinyl surface does not contact the instrument's finish.

5) Be careful when you put a banjo away with a capo in place. Some large capos will contact the case lid and place undue pressure against the neck.

6) Do not leave banjos in the heat — the neck will be the first thing to show signs of damage, with a warp or bow from excessive heat while under string pressure. Further, the finish could badly check or blush.

Bridges

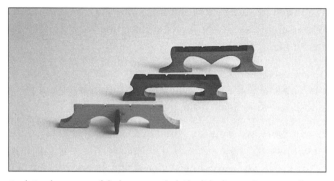

Emulating the structure of the human ear, the bridge links the string's energy to the banjo's sound producing membrane.

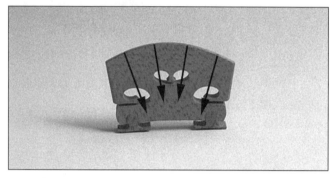

Fig. 5-1. The bridge of the viol family has evolved through centuries of development. Uniquely designed, there is no direct route for the strings' vibrations to reach the feet.

BACKGROUND OF THE BRIDGE

In the section on the human ear I mentioned that the ossicles — the three little bones inside the ear — provide the necessary connection between the ear drum and the inner ear (cochlea). The banjo's bridge is akin to these bones, except that the bridge is a single element. It is the bridge's duty and purpose to transmit the vibrations from the strings to the soundboard (head) and to do so without damping the vibrations or disturbing any of the tonal characteristics of the instrument.

Any further discussion of the bridge calls for some interesting background on the most classic movable bridge of all: the bridge of the viol family. It is interesting to note that this time-honored bridge was designed so that there was no direct route for any string's vibration to reach the soundboard (Fig. 5-1). All strings are positioned over an opening, and all energy is equally diverted to the soundboard via either the treble or the bass foot of the bridge.

The typical banjo bridge, especially the designs made popular by Grover, has some strings positioned directly over feet and others directly over spans, or "arches," in both the 4- and 5-string models. This direct or indirect routing of the strings' vibrations causes a major difference in dynamics from string to string.

I have experimented with dozens of bridge designs from 2-footed to 6-footed, some styled after the violin bridge with no direct route of vibrations to the soundboard, and others with independent feet for each string. I have tested bridges made from ebony, rosewood, plastic, aluminum, and even titanium. Each of these combinations imparts an unusual and different sound to the instrument, and all are open to conjecture as to which is "better." They are all different

from what we are used to. It wouldn't take long to adjust to the new tone colors these bridges provide, and it's really a matter of breaking the familiarity we all have with the sound produced by the conventional 3-footed bridge.

In the past few decades, some variations of the conventional bridge have developed. These primarily include bridges corrected for intonation, an important phenomenon that deserves further discussion. Intonation correction is the science of having all strings, regardless of gauge, note truly when fretted at all fret positions. The intonation problem occurs where heavier gauges of strings note sharper (higher pitch) than lighter gauges at the same fret. The difference in pitch occurs because the heavier gauges do not stretch as easily as the lighter gauges, and when pressed and stretched the same distance to the fretboard, the increased tension on the string — just to move it that slight distance to the fretboard — causes the pitch of the string to increase.

There are several ways to control this, and one is to use strings that all have identical tension while at pitch. String manufacturers attempt to compensate for this problem by using similar core wires with various sizes of wrap wire, but the *perfect* compensation and core/wrap selection cannot always be achieved. A detailed study on strings and a chart of string gauges and tensions at various tunings is provided for your reference in *Chapter 8, Strings.*

The traditional method of compensation for various string gauges is to modify the string *length* slightly at the bridge. Solidbody electric guitars boast bridges with adjustable string saddles so that each string's length can be adjusted to compensate for intonation problems (these are called "intonation compensated" or "intonation corrected" saddles). Various intonation corrected bridges have come

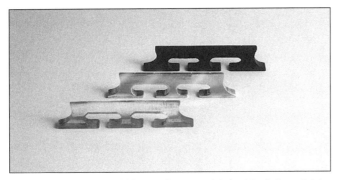

Fig. 5-2. The bridge is the main link between the strings and the head. Test bridges included those made from rosewood, aluminum, and acrylic plastic.

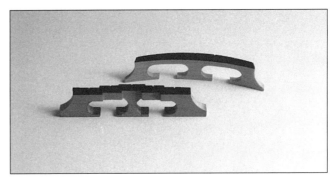

Fig. 5-3. Two examples of intonation corrected bridges. Both are heavier and bulkier than standard bridges.

on the market for banjo, and while they correct for intonation, they also present us with a more massive bridge. As you will soon learn, for a banjo bridge, less mass is desirable.

The most efficient way to correct for intonation with a straight bridge is to slant the bridge slightly counterclockwise, which will provide an acceptable intonation adjustment for the increasing mass of 1st, 2nd, 3rd and 4th strings. While this causes a minor problem for the 5th string — which should be of the same gauge as the 1st string — the 5th string is typically not fretted in all but melodic playing.

The mass (a combination of weight and size) of the bridge is very important for efficient transmission of the strings' vibrations to the soundboard. The bridge is merely a link between the strings and the head. If the bridge is too heavy, the strings will not be able to transmit their energy to the head. If the bridge is too light, it will damp the strings' vibrations, or worse, it will break.

Consider the analogy of driving nails with a hammer. You choose a hammer that has mass relative to the nail you are driving: big heavy hammers for common nails, and small tack hammers for brads. The relationship between string mass and bridge mass is quite similar. It's all an issue of inertia and the transfer of energy from one element to another.

From extensive tests, it appears that the weight of the bridge should not exceed one-half the weight of the strings. While I do not suggest that you perform this test and begin weighing your strings and bridges, I do offer the data for your information and to give you a better understanding of the relationship between the mass of the strings and the mass of the bridge. Here's the weight of a set of "RB" strings cut to their string scale lengths so that only the live portion of the string was weighed. (Just for reference, 1/8 ounce equals 54.7 grains.)

Note	Gauge	Weight (grains)
D	.010"	5 gr
B	.013"	6 gr
G	.014"	10 gr
D	.022"w	25 gr
G	.009"	4 gr
		50 gr

A 5/8" Grover 5-string bridge was weighed at 26 grains, making it basically one-half of the strings' weight. Of course, string gauges can be changed and/or the bridge can be thinned (to about 20 grains), which would improve its performance.

A key issue in bridge design is the position and quantity of bridge feet. As mentioned earlier in this section, the viol family bridge was designed such that no string has a direct route to the soundboard. This is not the case with bridges for our 4- and 5-string instruments, with some strings directly over feet and others over arches. This calls for some creative thinking in making string selections, such that lighter strings are used over feet and heavier strings are used over arches to balance and modulate the output. It also calls for designing the ideal banjo bridge with feet tuned to the size of the corresponding string, or all strings over an arch, or whatever else comes to mind.

The most wonderful feature about the banjo bridge is that it presents many opportunities for the creative mind. Bridges are relatively easy to make, easy to change, and the various designs have a great affect on the banjo's amplitude, tambre, and brightness. It may be well worth your time to experiment and see what you can come up with.

Today, Grover — the most popular brand — produces five models of bridges including the following: "Non-Tip" bridges with a fiber center support, "Leader" two-footed models, "Acousticraft" three-footed, ebony-topped bridges with "ivroid" inserts for each string, "Minstrel" conventional three-footed bridges with ebony top, and "Tune-Kraft" intonation compensated bridges (Fig. 5-4). These bridges are available in 1/2" and 5/8" — the 9/16" versions

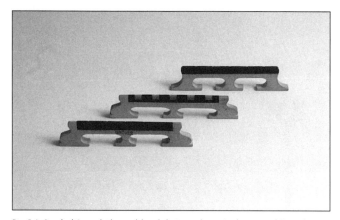

Fig. 5-4. Standard Grover bridge models include (top to bottom), ebony-topped Minstrel, Acousticraft with ivroid inserts, and an earlier variation of the Acousticraft model without the ivroid inserts.

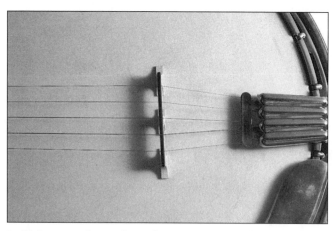

Fig. 5-5. One way to achieve an almost-perfect intonation is to turn the bridge counterclockwise slightly until the 1st string and 4th string are properly intonated.

are no longer available but easily made from the 5/8" bridge.

"But, which one is better?" you might ask. Pick the strings that are positioned over arches and the ones over feet, and listen to the difference. Then, do some whittling and develop a bridge that sounds right to you and matches your attack. That's the best one!

Improvements You Can Make

1. Correct Intonation Position (Relative to Fretboard). The bridge should first be positioned so that it is the same distance from the 12th fret as the nut is from the 12th fret. That is, when the bridge is in position, the 12th fret is exactly halfway between the nut and the bridge. Position the bridge first, by this measurement technique. Bring the strings up to pitch. To determine the exact location of the bridge, play the 1st string and then fret and play the 1st string at the 12th fret. The notes should be exactly one octave apart. If the fretted note sounds *sharp* (too high), the bridge is too close and it must be moved toward the tailpiece. If the fretted note sounds *flat* (too low), the bridge, is too far from the 12th fret and it should be moved toward the peghead. Try this again for the 4th string — you may find that the bridge has to be cocked at an angle to compensate for the needs of both the 4th string and the 1st string. See "#2, Intonation Correction (Turning the Bridge)," in the following section. Each time you move the bridge you must retune the strings. Once the bridge is in the right location, each string should note true to its octave when played in the open position and again at the 12th fret.

The preferred method for obtaining precise final position is to use harmonics. You can create a harmonic for each string by touching the string lightly directly above the 12th fret with the left hand, while picking it with the right hand. To hear the fretted octave note, press down on the string and fret it against the 12th fret and play it again. Those notes should sound exactly the same. If not, move the

bridge accordingly. Check the harmonics and fretted notes for the 1st through 4th strings. Check to see that the banjo is still in tune between adjustments.

NOTES

1) When moving the bridge, use both hands and apply pressure at both ends of the bridge. Grasp the bridge between thumb and forefinger — don't just push the bridge without supporting it in the upright position.

2) After each position change, you must retune the strings.

2. Intonation Correction (Turning the Bridge). Often, to get the correct intonation, the bridge will have to be turned counterclockwise so that the bridge-to-nut distance of the 4th string is greater than the bridge-to-nut distance of the 1st string (Fig. 5-5). Check each string by playing it in the open position and then playing the string fretted at the 12th fret. Those notes are one octave apart. Double check it with the harmonic method. If the fretted note is sharp, move the bridge back towards the tailpiece. If the fretted note is flat, move the bridge towards the peghead. Work the 1st and 4th string independent of the 2nd and 3rd strings. As with paragraph #1 above, angle and move the bridge until the 1st and 4th strings note correctly (the 2nd and 3rd strings should be correct at this time). Again, the preferred method for precise positioning of the bridge is to use harmonics as described in paragraph #1, above. However, using *both* harmonics and fretting the note is a great way to assure that you have achieved the correct position.

NOTE

During each position change you will have to retune the instrument.

You may find it impossible to achieve perfection on all strings. In all probability, you will get the 1st, 3rd and 4th strings to note true, and find that the 2nd string just doesn't want to cooperate. Study *Chapter 8, Strings* to determine if changing the string gauge will help.

3. Intonation Correction (Contact Points). The upper edge of the banjo bridge — usually made of an ebony strip — presents too small of an edge to correct for intonation by filing one side or another of the bridge's top. In addition, you need a sufficient width of ebony for structural integrity. However, you can easily glue a small piece of ebony to one side of the bridge and reshape the top using jewelers files to arrive at the desired intonation change for the 2nd and 3rd string.

Intonation-corrected bridges are available from various manufacturers and are very easy to install. However, the weight of the massive structure of most of these bridges, in my opinion, renders them less than ideal.

4. Correct Position (Relative to Head). This is a very important, and somewhat complicated adjustment. All soundboards vibrate in various modes and partials in much the same way strings do, and I review some of this science in *Chapter 6, Heads.*

For each soundboard — on every different instrument — there is an ideal and precise placement of the bridge, and such is the case for the banjo. On a round head, to get maximum brightness, the bridge should be located at a position on the head that is exactly 1/3 of the way across the head's *active* diameter. "Active" is the key word here: while an archtop tone chamber is 11" overall diameter, the active head area is 9-1/2". On an archtop banjo, therefore, the bridge should be located at a point that is 3.16" (slightly more than 3-1/8") from the active edge of the soundboard (head), or 3.91" from the outer edge of the rim (3.16" + .75" rim thickness). On the flathead instrument, the active area is actually about 10-3/4", which means that the bridge should be located at a point 3.58" (slightly more than 3-1/2") from the outer edge of the soundboard (head).

However, this does not occur in practice. Since the same fretting scale length is used for both archtop and flathead banjos, the bridge is virtually in the same place relative to the neck and pot assembly. Therefore, the bridge on most archtop models is anywhere from 3" to 3-3/8" from the inner edge of the soundboard, and 4" to 4-3/8" on flattop models. It is this difference in bridge locations (the *location of attack*), relative to the head's vibrational modes, that creates the major difference in sound and tambre between archtop and flattop banjos. This, coupled with the fact that the different sizes of the heads create a different tuning for each design, are the two key reasons flattops and archtops sound so different.

The lengths of banjo necks — specifically, the distance between the nut and the end of the fretboard — differ from various manufacturers and even differ from instrument to instrument from the same manufacturer. While the string scales may be the same, the way the end of the neck and fretboard are cut forces the bridge to be positioned at different points on the head.

Fig. 5-6. During one of our tests, the bridge was epoxied to the head to trap longitudinal vibrations. The outcome was different, slightly richer due to improved partials, but not necessarily better than unglued tests.

Getting the bridge positioned at the optimum position (1/3 the distance across the head) can be achieved on archtops but not on flattops. So, if you have an archtop banjo, you might want to consider the following "a)" and/or "b)" suggestions. If your banjo has a flattop tone chamber, skip to "5. Weight."

NOTE
Bear in mind that you cannot just move the bridge to the 1/3 point without disrupting the intonation point of the bridge. The bridge and fretboard have to move together. There are basically two ways of getting closer to a solution:

1) Locate the correct intonation point for the bridge, and measure where the feet need to be. If it is only a short distance — up to 1/8" — from where the bridge now is, you can adjust the angle of the foot of the bridge so that the bridge leans slightly, placing the contact point where it needs to be. Do not exceed an angle of 3° from vertical. If satisfied with the results, sand the bottom of the bridge feet so that the bottom of the feet match the desired angle.

2) The key determining factor of where the bridge ends up is how the neck heel was cut, and not all makers trim the length of the neck at the same distance from the 12th fret. As you might imagine, on any given neck, as the neck heel gets shorter, the bridge moves closer to the tailpiece and vice versa. If you are anxious to achieve this precise bridge contact point, the neck heel can be trimmed or shimmed as necessary according to which way you need to move the bridge. If it needs to be trimmed, this should be left only to a competent repairperson, since trimming also has an affect on neck angle. Shimming, on the other hand, is easy. Excellent shims can be made from brass, aluminum, or plastic shim stock that is shaped to match the neck heel, and drilled or punched for the lag screws or dowel sticks. Adjustments beyond 1/8" either way will be either impractical or impossible.

Fig. 5-7. The mass of the bridge can be decreased by removing material from its sides. The rounded end of a belt sander is helpful here.

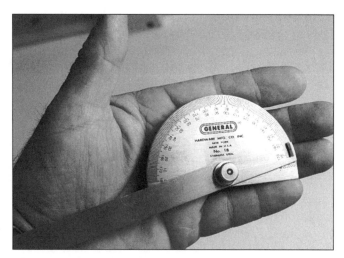

Fig. 5-8. String angles were measured with this commercially available metal protractor.

5. Weight. Conventional bridges can be sanded to make them thinner and lighter (Fig. 5-7). A great deal of weight can be removed from the waist of the bridge without disturbing thickness of the top or the feet. From an end view, the base should be wider than the top, giving added strength to the bridge, and keeping the mass near the soundboard (head). Further, wider feet help to distribute longitudinal vibrations which, while less important on the banjo, do contribute to the overall sound, and therefore, should be considered.

6. Structure (Height) and String Angle. Bridges are available in heights of 5/8" and 1/2". The 5/8" bridges are the most popular because: 1) they have the ideal mass, 2) they usually provide optimum string angle, 3) they offer ideal string-to-head space when playing the strings away from the bridge (playing near the fretboard excites lower numbered partials and provides a warmer tone — see *Chapter 2, How It Works*), and 4) they are typically high enough for the average playing feel.

9/16" bridges are no longer available but can be easily fabricated by adjusting the height of a 5/8" bridge (as can any height between 5/8" and 1/2", for that matter).

The desired string angle — that angle made by the string bent over the bridge — is 13° to 15° and is a very important feature to consider. String angle is further described in *Chapter 7, Tailpieces*. If the final setup of the instrument (with the tailpiece as low as it can go) does not allow for the correct string angle, a taller bridge will be necessary or possibly the neck height and/or neck angle should be changed (see *Chapter 4, Necks*). A string angle under 13° should be considered unacceptable. In the event you cannot locate a protractor (Fig. 5-8) or similar tool, make a pattern from this drawing of a 15° angle:

Once the height of the bridge is altered, the neck angle will also have to be changed to reset the action (the distance between the 12th fret and the strings). The angle can be increased or decreased through three adjustments: 1) recutting the neck heel, or 2) adding shims to the upper or lower part of the neck heel (see *Chapter 4, Necks*), and 3) adjusting the coordinator rods (see "Coordinator Rod Adjustment" in *Chapter 3, Pot Assemblies*).

Changing the neck height is a more complex matter and is described in *Chapter 4, Necks*, in the section entitled "Neck Height Adjustment."

7. Structure (Thickness). As previously described in "5. Weight," bridges can be easily thinned to make them lighter. This can be done by holding the bridge and sanding it against a piece of blocked sandpaper until the desired thickness is achieved. If you have a belt sander available to you, an ideal way to shape the bridge is to hold it against the roller part of the sander to remove wood from the waist of the bridge. What is the correct thickness? Trial and error is the ideal answer for your banjo, and this method calls for owning two bridges: the second one lets you do what you need to once you've sanded the first one too far.

8. Structure (Materials and Shapes). Because the bridge is so easily changeable, it offers an ideal scenario for experimentation. Shapes, openings, string inserts (protective string inserts imbedded into the ebony), number of feet, location of feet, size of feet, intonation changes, and materials are but a few easily changeable items to experiment with (Figs. 5-9 and 5-10). Be creative! Experiment!

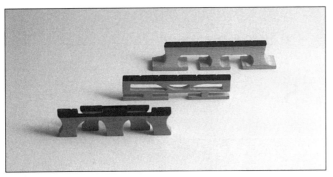

Fig. 5-9. Extreme changes in tone and amplitude were noted with these bridges. Top to bottom: extra-heavy maple/ebony bridge (softened the tone and excessively damped the amplitude), violin-type bridge with no direct route to the feet (excellent string-to-string balance, but somewhat muted and mellow), and a two piece bridge with separate feet for each string (excellent string-to-string balance but tricky to set up and maintain position).

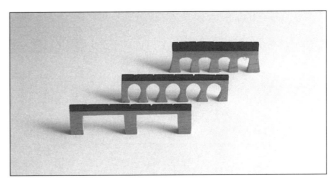

Fig. 5-10. Top to bottom, these bridges were designed to position strings over feet, strings over arches, and an ultralight bridge. All presented interesting and different results, leaving the final decision to personal tastes.

9. String Selection Relative to Bridge Feet. *Chapter 8, Strings*, talks about string tensions relative to each string's position over a bridge foot or arch. The charts provided in that section offer string tensions for a range of strings that are capable of producing each note. For example: the 5-string "RB" banjo chart shows five different string gauges capable of producing the *G* and *D*, six strings capable of producing the *B*, six capable of producing the *G*, and nine capable of producing the *D* (in wound and plain combinations). Although the methods of attack are different for 5-string "RB" banjos and for Tenor and Plectrum banjos, greater balance will be achieved by selecting the greater tensions for strings that rest over the bridge arch (where there is no direct route to the soundboard [head]) and lesser tensions for strings that rest directly over the bridge feet (where there is a direct route to the soundboard).

Use the string tension tables when selecting strings. If a given set does not have the gauge you seek, ask for single string selections (many manufacturers offer string gauge kits so you can choose any gauge you desire) and make up your own sets. This is a very inexpensive, simple, and fruitful way of altering the tonal characteristics of your instrument.

10. Bridge Feet Relative to String Selection. Here's the flip side of the previous paragraph. You may want to consider altering the mass of the bridge feet under each string. To do this, consider modifying a three-footed bridge whose two outer feet have been reduced in size and whose center foot remains untouched. Strive for a balance between string choice (tension and mass) and bridge design.

Maintenance Tips

1) On bridges with ebony tops, inspect the string notches frequently to assure that the notches have not widened or the ebony has not checked or fractured.

2) Carry an extra bridge in your instrument case.

Heads

The head provides a window for the banjo to connect its magical voice to the surrounding environment.

Fig. 6-1. Skin heads became easier to install once they were available pre-fitted to the "flesh hoop."

The earliest heads were made of calfskin and were very susceptible to changes in the weather. When the humidity was high, the head would absorb moisture, become more supple, and stretch, resulting in a loss of the instrument's brightness. When the weather was dry, the banjo head became tighter, which improved brightness but also lead to head cracking.

By the mid '30s, the leading head manufacturers, such as Ludwig and Jos. B Rogers Jr., developed methods for impregnating the heads with wax and other sealants to prevent it from absorbing moisture, and many of these treated natural skin heads are still in playable condition today.

The earliest skin heads were sold as flat, unmounted circles, approximately 14" in diameter (for an 11" head). The mounting process included wetting the skin until it was soft (in much the same way a dry automotive chamois is stiff until fully wetted) and laying it over the rim and tone chamber. The flesh hoop (a brass ring around which the outer edge of the head was held) was then placed around the head and down over tone chamber. Then, the stretcher band was installed while the skin was pulled up between the rim and the stretcher band. Most manufacturers provided a set of four extra-long hooks to use until the stretcher band (now you see where it gets its name) was pulled down far enough to use the standard hooks. Once all the extra skin was pulled up, everything was jockeyed around until the flesh hoop was level and almost-equal pieces of skin were protruding up. Then came the magic: the installer had to have a good sense about how much the head could be stretched before reaching its proper tightness point to have the stretcher band end up in the right

place. Finally, when the head was stretched, the excess skin was cut off with a razor or sharp knife against the inside of the stretcher band (ever wonder what those fine scratches were around the inside of stretcher bands on earlier instruments?). Anyway, the whole process wasn't fun!

As the early tone chamber designs were developed, it became obvious that the head always dried slower, if at all, in that little space between the first bearing ring (a round brass rod set on the outer top edge of the rim of some early models to provide a good turning and bearing surface for the skin head) and the outer edge of the rim, since only one side of the skin was open to the air in that area. This made some heads prone to rot along that edge. Drilled tone tubes provided ventilation to this area and stimulated equal drying.

In the mid 1930s, skin heads were formed to shape and pre-attached to their flesh hoops — a major boon for banjo players everywhere.

Stemming from the technological developments of World War II, a very durable polyester film material called "Mylar" was developed by "ICI" in Scotland in the early '50s, and later licensed to DuPont. Working in New Mexico in 1957, Chick Evans developed methods for using Mylar for drum heads, and shortly thereafter, Los Angeles-based Remo Belli advanced the art of attaching the Mylar to the supporting rings, or "flesh hoops." By the end of the decade, both Evans and Remo heads became highly popular for drum and banjo heads. The Mylar heads were produced in numerous varieties of film including white, translucent-white, clear, amber-clear, and semi-clear, and

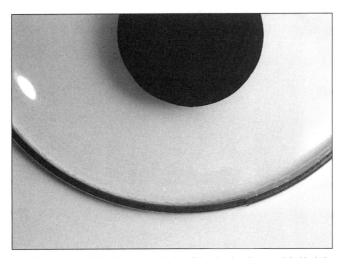

Fig. 6-2. In the early 1980s, Remo produced a line of drum heads with a special double thick contact spot in the center. We had one made up for banjo tests with the spot under the bridge. The extra thickness robbed amplitude but provided a very mellow tonal characteristic.

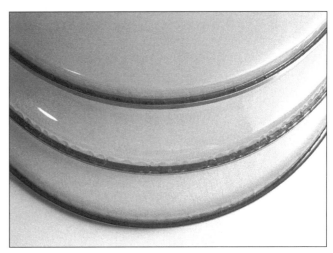

Fig. 6-3. Difficult to appreciate from photos, Mylar for non-sprayed heads is available (top to bottom) translucent, crystal clear, and milk white. Of these, the translucent seems to provide the best overall tone.

several textured and grained versions were evaluated. To make them look more skin-like, head manufacturers such as Remo sprayed the heads with a matte white lacquer. Spray coatings varied from manufacturer to manufacturer and from the periods in which they were made, and the rough, coarse heads were the least acceptable due to the thickness of the coating. Fine coatings — those in which you cannot feel the texture of the paint — are best and, generally, the sprayed heads provide a warmer richer tone compared to clear heads, which tend to produce brighter tones.

For reference, here is a listing of thickness for several types of heads. While skin heads are no longer manufactured for banjos, I have included two types of Jos B. Rogers Jr. skin heads just for comparison:

Jos B Rogers, std	.016″
Jos B Rogers, "Minstrel" brand	.012″
heavy sprayed, on Mylar	.011″
moderate sprayed, on Mylar	.009″
amber-clear	.007″
crystal clear	.0065″

For most tastes, the moderately sprayed heads measuring .009″ to .010″ seem to provide the best dynamics and balance between amplitude and tone.

Anything on the head will weigh it down and reduce its ability to generate bright clear tones. It's like putting a piece of tape on a bell. Aside from the thickness or composition, the magic comes from "tuning" the head to the correct pitch in much the same way drummers tune their drums. This tuning process is very important to the overall tone of the banjo. There is a different tuning needed for flathead and archtop banjos because of the difference in the area (size) of their vibrating surfaces. For each tone chamber design, the Mylar will be brought to roughly the same tension, but the pitch will be different because of the

difference in area of the two tone chamber systems. The entire tuning process is described in detail in *Chapter 9, Tuning the Assembly.*

Another important issue is the amount of load placed on the head by the bridge and tailpiece combined (see *Chapter 7, Tailpieces*). This "loading" is a critical element to the amplitude and tonal character of the banjo. Too light a load (where, for example, the strings pass almost straight over the bridge to the tailpiece with little or no string angle over the bridge) presents a mismatch between the head's surface tension and the bridge's downward pressure, and the instrument would generate little or no sound. Too severe a load (where, for example, a severe string angle over the bridge forces the head into a very visible depression in the head) constrains the head in its ability to vibrate freely, resulting in the amplitude being greatly suppressed. Excessive pressure also raises the pitch of the head beyond the target tunings.

There is a stasis or balance that is reached between the bridge's down pressure and the head's surface tension to resist that down pressure. Basically, the strings (and bridge) push down until they are met by an equal resistance from the pushing up of the head, whose stiffness or starting point was first established by *tuning* the head, and both reach a stasis and come to rest. The head can now vibrate both up and down in response to the tensioning and de-tensioning of the strings as they vibrate to produce sound.

Improvements You Can Make

1. Head Selection. There is a wide variety of heads to choose from. Clear heads usually sound brighter than sprayed ones, and translucent heads are somewhere in between. As we have learned in *Chapter 3, Pot Assemblies,* flattops are usually warmer than archtops. So, if you are

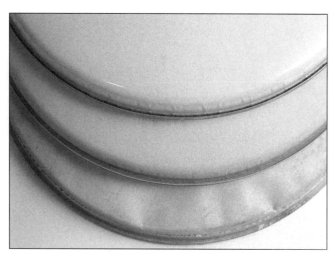

Fig. 6-4. Top to bottom: opal (clear, amber-ish) heads have excellent tonal qualities. Many players still prefer the sprayed version (Scruggs prefers his as heavily sprayed as possible). And, of course, the skin heads are great for old-time and frailing banjos.

Fig. 6-5. Heavily sprayed heads provide a comparatively "dark" tone. These can be made a bit brighter by removing some of the excess coating. Sanding lightly with 400-grit sandpaper will remove some of the surface.

going for bell-like brightness, combine a clear head with an archtop. If you want to brighten a very warm flattop, give it a clear head. If you want to mellow down a bright archtop, use a sprayed head, and so on.

Also, you can adjust the brightness of the head you select when you tune the instrument as described in *Chapter 9, Tuning the Assembly.*

2. Tightness. The head should be very tight, but just "how tight?" is always the question. Ideally, you will choose to tune the head as described in *Chapter 9, Tuning the Assembly.* If you have problems with the process, or if you just cannot hear the head being tuned to a pitch (which takes a little practice), then tighten the head so that the nuts are reasonably snug. With the coarse-threaded (8x26) hooks, that would be enough for you to feel sufficient thumb and forefinger pressure on the T-wrench — about as much as turning a really stubborn automotive ignition key to the start position. With 8x32 threads, there is greater mechanical advantage, so you have to be a little more delicate. It's surprising how easy it is to tear the Mylar head from its "flesh hoop." The head should be tightened so that you can snap your fingernail on it and get a healthy "pop."

However, there really is no substitute for tuning, and unless you have a really bad ear cold and just can't hear, I suggest you spend the time learning the tap-tuning process described in *Chapter 9, Tuning the Assembly.*

3. Reducing Mass. On sprayed heads, you can reduce the mass of the head by lightly sanding the top of the head with 400 sandpaper. If you do this in large sweeping motions, you will not leave any marks. Sand just to where you see the white paint becoming translucent. Removing just a little bit of mass (paint) can make a big difference.

CAUTION
If you go too far, you cannot undo your sanding.

NOTE
If you plan to "tune" the head as described in Chapter 9, Tuning the Assembly, *sand the head first, since reducing mass from the head will increase its pitch and alter its tuning.*

4. Installation. Mylar heads are a snap to install, and I assume that you know how to disassemble your banjo. It is best to put the head in place, assure that the tone chamber and flanges are properly aligned for neck fit, install the stretcher band and get the neck notch properly lined up (not a bad idea to position the neck temporarily in the pot assembly until everything is snug), and put on four brackets at four different quadrants around the head. Snug these up but do not tighten them. Install all brackets and proceed around the rim, tightening each nut one-half turn until the head comes up to pitch. See "2. Tightness" above, for bringing the head to a playable point and *Chapter 9, Tuning the Assembly,* for tuning the head to the correct pitch.

Maintenance Tips

1) Although Mylar is a very stabile material, it is wise to check the tuning or tightening of the head at least once a year.

2) Mylar banjo heads can be safely cleaned with Windex, 409, or similar detergents.

3) For Tenor and Plectrum players still using skin heads, keep them away from moisture or excessive dryness.

Tailpieces

These stalwart guardians ensure that the strings' tensions and complex angles are securely maintained.

The earliest tailpieces were small bracket-like stampings and rings around which the string would be tied or looped. A wide variety of tailpieces have followed: hinged-cover and plain, adjustable or fixed, cast and stamped, and in a wide range of metal gauges from substantial-and-heavy to much-too-light.

The tailpiece became a highly decorated part of many models, and some featured hinged covers to protect the player's garments from the barbs of carelessly tied string ends. There was also a wide array of designs, shapes, and openings to hold the strings in place at the bridge end of the tailpiece. But above all, the length and substance of the tailpiece was important.

As technology developed, it was found that the tailpiece was an important part of the banjo's acoustical system, and not just a string harness. More important than holding one end of the string, it was learned that three other elements contributed greatly to the amplitude and tambre of the instrument: 1) the amount of down pressure the tailpiece could provide behind the bridge to push the strings down to the head, 2) the length of the tailpiece — the distance from the bridge to the contact point at the tailpiece (the length was critical for balancing the amplitude and brightness of the instrument, as this distance controls the extent of the bridge's movement), and 3) the stiffness of the tailpiece — its resistance to springing up and down with the strings' movements.

Down pressure increases with string angle. To measure the pressure, a standard set of D'Addario RB banjo strings were brought to pitch and tested in a fixture using a certified Dillion tension gauge (Figs. 7-1 and 7-2). The fol-lowing chart demonstrates the differences in down pressures at various degrees of string angle:

String angle	Pressure (pounds)
0°	0
3°	3
6°	7
9°	10.5
12°	13.5
15°	18

The final string angle is determined by several adjustments: neck angle (see *Chapter 4, Necks*), bridge height (see *Chapter 5, Bridges*), head tension — more specifically, how deep of a depression the bridge will make into the head under tension (see *Chapter 6, Heads*), and tailpiece length and down angle (this chapter).

Improvements You Can Make

1. Down Pressure. One critical job of the tailpiece is to exert down pressure on the bridge to force the strings and bridge against the banjo's head. As discussed in *Chapter 6, Heads*, for the instrument to work effectively, the head must be "loaded" by this down pressure. This "loading" is a critical element to the banjo's sound. Too light of a load caused by the strings passing straight over the bridge to the tailpiece with no string angle over the bridge would direct little or no energy down to the head, and amplitude (volume) and tone would suffer greatly. Too severe of a load causes an extreme string angle over the bridge and constrains the head's ability to vibrate freely, making amplitude and tone suffer. (Fortunately, on most banjos, it's difficult to arrive at a string angle that exceeds 15°.)

As discussed in *Chapter 5, Heads*, there is a stasis or balance that is reached between the string/bridge down pressure and the head's resistance of that down pressure. The strings and bridge push down until they are met by an equal resistance from the head, whose stiffness or starting point was first established by *tuning* the head, and both reach a stasis and come to rest. The head can now vibrate both up and down in response to the strings' tensioning and de-tensioning as they vibrate to produce sound. While the amount of loading is established by the height of the bridge and angle of the neck, the final controlling factor is determined by the length of the tailpiece and the amount of down pressure it can apply behind the bridge.

Fig. 7-1. To measure the down pressure at various string angles, this fixture features a 26″ string scale and a "bridge" supported by a certified Dillion tension gauge. As the gauge (and bridge) is raised, the angle to the tailpiece increases and the resultant load is measured. Here a 6° angle indicates 7 pounds of load.

Fig. 7-2. As the "bridge" cradle is raised, the string angle and down pressure increases. At 15° the gauge reads 18 pounds.

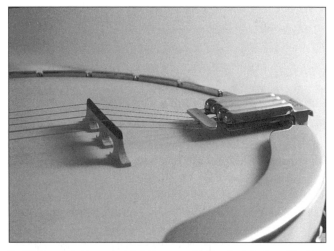

Fig. 7-3. The correct string angle at the bridge assures that the strings' vibrations will be driven to the head and not absorbed by the tailpiece. Some stamped tailpieces don't have the fortitude for lots of down pressure.

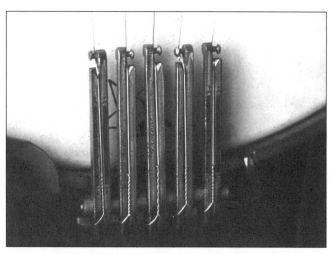

Fig. 7-4. Fred Bacon of Bacon & Day designed this unique tailpiece with individually adjustable fingers for each string. These tailpieces, especially the 5-string versions, are a rare find and provide excellent adjustment control. OME still provides similar tailpieces.

As previously stated, the ideal "string break" or "string angle" is between 13° and 15°. A diagram of that string angle can be found in *Chapter 5, Bridges*, under "Improvements You Can Make," in the section entitled "6. Structure (Height) and String Angle."

2. Length of Tailpiece. The length of the tailpiece has a great deal to do with achieving the desired string angle. The key question is, "just how long should it be?"

Long versions, such as the early Kershner and similar tailpieces with a reach of 2-1/2" to 2-3/4", work very well and provide excellent leverage and stability (Fig. 7-5).

Short Grover-type tailpieces have a reach of about 2", and even if the neck is set up at an extreme angle and a 9/16" bridge is used, this tailpiece might not have sufficient reach to provide the desired string angle (Fig. 7-7).

As pointed out in *Chapter 5, Bridges*, there is an optimal position for the bridge, and we have determined that to be at a point 1/3 of the way across the head. In this regard, bridges sitting on a flattop tone chamber (which has an active surface diameter of 10-3/4") are not in the same location relative to the vibrational modes of the head as those sitting on an archtop tone chamber with an active surface diameter of 9-1/2". While the difference is slight, it is still one of those things to consider and may suggest that a different tailpiece should be used.

Generally speaking, longer tailpieces produce sharp, brighter, snappier tones, and the converse is true of shorter tailpieces. This suggests that longer tailpieces could be used on a flathead banjo to brighten its somewhat mellower sound. Shorter tailpieces also provide a bit more sustain than longer ones do, as they permit greater flexibility behind the bridge.

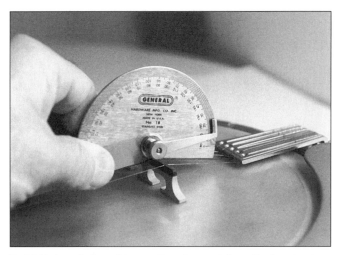

Fig. 7-5. The heavy Kershner tailpieces provide excellent muscle for cranking down the strings behind the bridge. This setup achieved a whopping 18°.

Fig. 7-6. In addition to the Kershner's heavy frame, the long arm helps get to the right string angle.

Fig. 7-7. For years, Grover made tons of these tailpieces with and without hinges, and with scalloped and oval openings (shown here). These tailpieces are very sturdy but a bit shorter than desirable.

Fig. 7-8. Some of the very early tailpieces, such as Loar's early TB-5, offered an attaching spot for the strings but zero down pressure.

Fig. 7-9. The Presto tailpieces were very popular on many makes of banjos. They are long, reasonably adjustable, and stamped of thick gauge brass.

Fig. 7-10. Simple adjustments can be made to arrive at greater string angles. This standard Gibson tailpiece yielded a 12° angle.

Fig. 7-11. By bending the front lip of the tailpiece down (in a padded vise), string angle increased to 14°.

Fig. 7-12. On the other end of the scale are these cheap tailpieces. They make great doorstops.

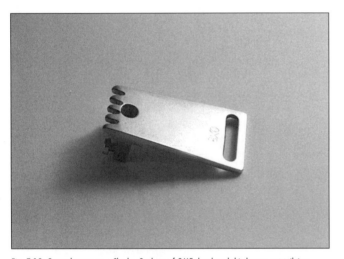

Fig. 7-13. Several years ago, Charles Ogsbury of OME developed this heavy cast tailpiece. It provided excellent stability, but the single screw design offered no downward adjustability (two screws offered rotational adjustment). Today OME features Presto-styles, and "bearclaw" tailpieces similar to the Bacon design in Fig. 7-4.

Fig. 7-14. This heavy Stelling tailpiece offers great stability and down pressure adjustment.

Another issue to consider is how much a long tailpiece might constrain the bridge's movement. If the tailpiece comes very close to the bridge, it will greatly hamper the amplitude (loudness), even if the correct string angle is achieved. For optimum results, there should be no less than 1-7/8" clear space between the bridge and the end of the tailpiece.

3. Angle of the Tailpiece. The angle of the tailpiece itself, that is, the degrees the tailpiece is angled down towards the head, is not important. The important angle is from the tailpiece up to and over the bridge (Figs. 7-10 and 7-11).

4. Structure of the Tailpiece. Practically all tailpieces are made of stamped or cast brass — brass is easy to cast, form, and machine, and it polishes and plates well. The durability of brass, however, especially when work-hardened (where bending it or changing its shape also changes its molecular structure in its bends), may occasionally fatigue and render

it fragile, and some tailpieces have been known to crack at the severe bend where the tailpiece lays over the stretcher band. Old, valuable tailpieces can be brazed and replated if done by skilled metal technicians, but they still may end up being incapable of handling the force needed for greater down pressure.

As a general rule of thumb, the heavier and more substantial the tailpiece is, the less it will damp vibrations and the better it will be. So, usually, heavier is better. "Just what is heavy?" On a stamped tailpiece, the brass should measure no less than .080" thick.

To test the stiffness of the tailpiece, play the strings and bounce your finger up and down on the end of the tailpiece. It should *not* be very easy for you to alter the strings' pitch. If you can, consider replacing the tailpiece with a heavier one.

Fig. 7-15. Gibson's popular "clamshell" tailpiece was manufactured in four bumps (shown), two bumps, and one bump according to year and model. Under the hinged cover, stampings in the base will accept ball-end or loop-end strings.

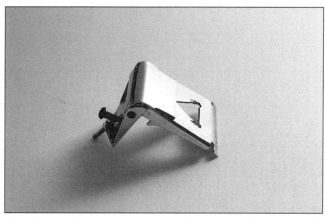

Fig. 7-16. Covered and plain, hinged or fixed, scores of other tailpieces like this one make tail-piece-gazing interesting.

5. Buzzes and Rattles. A major source of tailpiece noise occurs between the tailpiece cover and base. This is usually due to the fact that not all tailpiece covers are spring loaded or latching, and they will rattle against other metal surfaces. An easy way to quiet them is to apply a thin piece of felt to the underside of the lid. Using chenille-covered (fuzz) loop-end strings will help, too.

6. Shapes and Designs. This is mostly a cosmetic consideration, and the important issue here is how easy it is to change strings — that is, getting the string fed through the tailpiece holes, under the "fingers," and looping in the end of the string. Aside from covered or plain, nickel or gold, stamped or cast, the key is in the stability, the length, and the ability to crank the tailpiece down to get the right string angle.

Maintenance Tips

1) All metal parts should be cleaned once a year to remove dirt and oxidation. Any of the jewelry polishes work well on these sensitive finishes.

2) Do not machine buff gold parts. Gold is plated over nickel and can be buffed through with little effort.

3) Some gold parts have a clear lacquer coating which can be damaged by some cleaners. Try a spot under a flange or on one of the attaching angle-brackets before cleaning a readily visible surface.

Strings

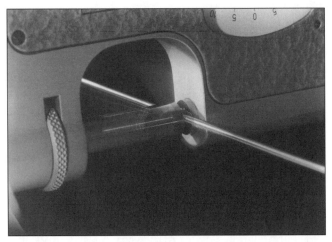

Like lanky translators, the strings communicate the artist's energy to the banjo's complex acoustical system.

BACKGROUND OF MUSICAL STRINGS

No one really knows who discovered the musical magic of a vibrating string, but it may have been the same caveman who invented the bow.

Even the most primitive early civilizations recognized that a tightened vine or rope could produce sounds. Early sailors must have marveled at the sound in their rigging lines set alive by the wind. And, early stone carvings indicate that stringed musical instruments were already a well developed part of human culture by 1500 BC. The famous Greek mathematician and philosopher Pythagoras, who died around 497 BC, laid the foundation for modern acoustical physics, and his theories about string vibration have held up for 2,500 years.

The principle behind the musical string is an ageless phenomenon of physics and not an invention. A tightened cord, when struck or plucked, will continue to vibrate until its energy is exhausted. As it vibrates, it will cause the air around it to move. If it is attached to a membrane such as a banjo head, larger masses of air will move. That air movement translates into waves of sound pressure which carry to our ears and trigger our sense of hearing.

The earliest conventional strings were made from gut with metal windings and appeared as early as 1880. Plain steel strings followed shortly thereafter, but their metal content was poor and strings were prone to breakage. At first, metal strings were only available with plain ends to be twisted and looped by the owner. It wasn't until the early 1930s that strings were manufactured with twisted loops at one end and in 1932, the brass ball-end string was announced.

The "Vibration of Strings" section in *Chapter 2, How It Works*, describes how strings vibrate and produce sound. It is important to add that in order to produce the wide range of notes demanded by any given instrument, both the gauge and the mass of the string is important. A gauge is the measurement of the string's thickness given in thousandths of an inch, millimeters, or both (as a cross-reference). The mass is a measurement of its weight and size taken as a whole and is important when we consider the different combinations of gauges used for wound stings.

GAUGES

There are several reasons that strings are available in a wide range of gauges. The fundamental reason is the note required from a specific length string at a given tension to drive a specified sound-producing system. Additionally: 1) Various instruments sound better when fitted with a particular gauge and type of strings, as in the case of the nylon strings common to classical guitars and the steel strings used on conventional acoustic guitars. 2) Some gauges and types of strings have a different affect on electromagnetic pickups and reproduce better electronically than others (i.e. bronze wound vs steel wound). 3) Various manufacturers and artists have personal preferences for what makes up the ideal or "balanced" set. 4) The combination of gauges needed for unusual bridge systems (as in the banjo, which has some strings resting directly over a bridge foot and others resting over the arched footless area). 5) The type and size of soundboards and associated air chambers that need to be driven by the strings. 6) The musical range of the instrument. 7) The system that will excite or drive the strings (bowed, plucked, hammered, etc.). 8) Finally, the issue of "feel," where musicians have preference for what is easier to play or "choke;" the lighter gauge strings being easier to play (they offer less resistance) than the heavier gauges.

MASS

A thin string will vibrate faster than a thick one when both are at the same tension. Light strings can move more rapidly, and faster vibration rates produce higher tones. That's why your banjo has its thinnest strings in the treble register and its thickest strings in the bass register.

As the mass (size and weight taken together) of a string increases, the rate at which it is able to vibrate decreases. Low note strings don't need to vibrate as fast as high note strings, and by weighting them down, we can decrease their speed. The trick is to give low note strings the right

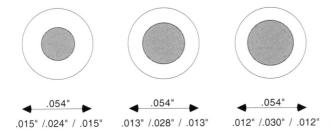

.054"
.015" /.024" / .015"   .054"
.013" /.028" / .013"   .054"
.012" /.030" / .012"

Fig. 8-1. The same size string can be made in many combinations of core and wrap wire. Here are three examples of how a .054" guitar string can be made.

Fig. 8-2. String tension (as opposed to down pressure) is measured in this fixture. Here, the Dillion gauge (out of the scene, to the left) is used at the end of the string to measure tension in pounds. This dial-indicator (gauge) is mounted on a steel rod that moves with the Dillion gauge. As the string is tightened up to pitch, the gauge measures the amount of string stretch in thousandths of an inch. The arrow indicates where the string is clamped to the gauge.

amount of mass without making them hard to play. To achieve this, string engineers use a thin core or center wire and wrap it with a second wire to add mass. It is the core wire that is brought up to tension — the wrap wire is there to add weight and produce a lower note.

Many combinations of wire gauges can be used to achieve the same overall string diameter. Figure 8-1 shows three core-and-wrap combinations each making up a .054" (fifty-four thousandths) string. Each of the combinations shown in Figure 8-1 could produce an acceptable low *E* string for the guitar, but each will have different characteristics of sound and playing "feel."

To provide a snug fit of the wrap wire onto the core wire, manufacturers use a core wire that is not perfectly round, called "hex core." The corners of the hexagonal core wire provide a better bite when the wrap wire is applied and prevent it from slipping back around the core. This is also helpful in preventing premature unraveling in the event a wrap wears through from excessive string-to-fret contact.

Hex core wire is a necessary evil. While the core must be shaped for a secure wrap, its flatted sides do not allow for as pure an orbit of the strings lateral vibrations as round wire does. That is, the hex wire tends to vibrate in the direction parallel to its flattest side. Envision this example: if you had a 12' length of 2"x4" lumber, secured at either end, and you struck it in the center with a hammer, would it vibrate back and forth in favor of the 2" or 4" faces? How would that compare to a 12' length of 2" or 4" *round dowel* lumber? In previous chapters we have talked about lateral and longitudinal vibrations and have come to learn that the lateral vibrations are important on the banjo. What if some of those vibrations are directed laterally — across

the bridge — rather than up and down at the bridge? Unfortunately, hex core wire (for wound strings) is another fact of banjo life to be reckoned with.

STRETCH AND ELASTICITY

Stretch is another factor that must be considered in the life of musical strings. Because musical wire is elastic, strings stretch as they are brought up to pitch. The amount of "give" or stretch that a piece of steel wire has is critical to the quality of its musical sound and to the longevity of its musical life.

Unlike a rubber band, steel wire continues to stretch until it elongates or ruptures. Musical wire, that which the industry refers to as "mandolin wire," has elastic properties that allow it to be slackened almost back to its original length. As strings age and are played — a factor that exhausts their elasticity — they lose their brightness and eventually need to be replaced.

The fixture shown in Fig. 8-2 demonstrates how the string's stretch can be measured. In this example the string tested was a .010" gauge which is intended as a *D* for 5-string banjo first string, a *D* for a Tenor second string, or the *D* for the Plectrum's first string. The sample .010" string stretched about .012" for every pound of tension until it finally ruptured at 22 pounds. Of course, as the string gauge gets heavier, the amount of stretch decreases per pound of tension.

Strings stretch and lose much of their elasticity in the first several hours after they are strung. This is why new strings are so bright and lively (and are prone to buzzes and rattles) and why they go out of tune so quickly. As strings are played, especially after several hours of heavy playing, the elasticity in the wire begins to fade. Notice that you always tighten new strings *up* to pitch — the direct result of the strings' stretching and generating more slack. Further, once the elasticity disappears, strings hold their pitch rather well. And finally, when all the elasticity is gone, strings sound "dead" and "dull." So, the idea of stretch and elasticity are important factors to understand, and something about which we have little control. (I know of some musicians who slack their strings after playing to maintain the string's brightness. They also suggest that this keeps their instruments sounding more consistent and lessens the need for string changes. However, I don't recommend it because it is more time consuming than changing strings once a month, but it's worth passing the idea on to you.)

The stretch factor based on strung-in-the-case time and performance time should be considered in the selection of the ideal string gauge, for it is the barometer of string life. Unfortunately, string manufacturers and private label marketers have not addressed the issue of elasticity, and very little data is readily available on the subject. Generally, we all agree that strings stretch, lose brightness, and need to be changed. Until more data becomes available on string packages and literature, the best we can do is recognize that for musicians, string changing is a fact of life.

TENSION

Musicians are always looking for a "balanced set" of strings. However, a balanced set can be several things: 1) one which has the same feel for both the right and left hand (that is, for fretting/choking action as well as for picking pressure), 2) one in which each of the strings comes up to pitch at similar or identical tensions, 3) one in which the strings exert equal energy to the soundboard (head), such that each string has equal dynamics (this issue is also discussed in *Chapter 5, Bridges*, where we have some strings resting directly over a bridge foot and others over a bridge arch) and finally, 4) one in which there is excellent string-to-string intonation — that is, each of the strings notes true with equal fretting pressure.

In the early 1980s, while doing research at *Frets Magazine*, I spearheaded a program for manufacturers to provide string tension on their packaging. Gibson was the first to comply, and many other manufacturers including D'Addario rallied to the cause to provide this valuable information (as of this writing, only D'Addario provides both gauge and tension specs on its Web site). In the absence of specific data or test equipment, one can only make this decision by feel, and to help you, I have provided a set of tension charts for selecting strings for "RB," Tenor, and Plectrum in this chapter.

Gauge	G Fifth	D Fourth	G Third	B Second	D First	Core/Wrap
.008"	9.40				9.40	
.009"	11.20			7.80	11.20	
.010"	13.00			9.00	13.00	
.011"	16.20			11.50	16.20	
.012"	19.30			13.30	19.30	
.013"			10.70	16.40		
.014"			12.00	18.40		
.015"		8.40	15.30	21.00		
.016"		8.60	15.60			
.018" P		10.80	18.60			
.018" W		10.30	18.40			.011"/ 004"
.020" P		13.30				
.020" W		11.70	21.10			.012"/.004"
.022" W		15.50				.014"/.004"
.024" W		18.80				.016"/.004"
.026" W		21.20				.016"/.005"

Fig. 8-3. This chart indicates the string tension in pounds for the various gauges used on a 5-string "RB" banjo. The tensions were measured on a 26" string scale.

To begin our discussion on tension, here is an example of the string tensions from three random sets (various manufacturers) of banjo strings:

5-string (RB) banjo, 26" string scale:

1st, *D*	2nd, *B*	3rd, *G*	4th, *D*	5th, *G*
.010"	.013"	.014"	.022"w	.009"
13 lbs	16 lbs	12 lbs	15 lbs	11 lbs

Total load (tension): 67 lbs

4-string Plectrum banjo, 26" string scale

1st, *D*	2nd, *B*	3rd, *G*	4th, *C*
.010"	.013"	.016"	.024"w
13 lbs	16 lbs	15 lbs	14 lbs

Total load (tension): 58 lbs

4-string Tenor banjo, 22-3/4" scale:

1st, *A*	2nd, *D*	3rd, *G*	4th, *C*
.009"	.011"	.018"w	.030"w
18 lbs	15 lbs	14 lbs	15 lbs

Total load (tension): 60 lbs

While the example above shows a different gauge string for the 1st and 5th string in the 5-string "RB" banjo set, many sets contain the same gauge for both the 1st and 5th strings. This is preferred, as both strings would be at equal tension when tuned to their respective notes.

To get a better idea of how string tensions come into play, see the gauge/tension charts in Fig. 8-3, Fig. 8-4, and Fig. 8-5.

Gauge	C Fourth	G Third	B Second	D First	Core/Wrap
.008"				9.40	
.009"			7.80	11.20	
.010"			9.00	13.00	
.011"			11.50	16.20	
.012"			13.30	19.30	
.013"		10.70	16.40		
.014"		12.00	18.40		
.015"		15.30	21.00		
.016"		15.60			
.018" P	8.70	18.60			
.018" W	8.60	18.40			.011"/.004"
.020" P	10.60				
.020" W	9.50	21.10			.012"/.004"
.022" W	12.30				.014"/.004"
.024" W	14.20				.016"/.004"
.026" W	16.70				.016"/.005"
.028" W	18.70				

Fig. 8-4. Here are the tensions for Plectrum banjo strings. These tensions were measured on a 26" string scale.

Gauge	C Fourth	G Third	D Second	A First	Core/Wrap
.008"				13.70	
.009"			8.50	18.10	
.010"			10.10	21.70	
.011"			12.60		
.012"			15.10		
.013"		8.40	17.00		
.014"		9.40	18.70		
.015"		11.00			
.016"		12.30			
.018" P	6.80	14.70			
.018" W	6.50	14.30			.011"/.004"
.020" P	8.30	17.50			
.020" W	7.40	16.50			.012"/.004"
.022" P	9.90				
.022" W	9.60				.014"/.004"
.024" W	11.20				.016" / .004"
.026" W	13.10				.016" / .005"
.028" W	14.60				.016" / .006"
.030" W	15.10				.016" / .007"
.032" W	17.70				.018" / .007"

Fig. 8-5. This listing contains tensions for Tenor banjo strings on a 22-3/4" string scale.

FACTORS TO CONSIDER WHEN REVIEWING THE TABLES

- In each test, I have not considered loads (tension) below 8 lbs of pull or those in excess of 22 pounds. For all strings in the banjo ranges (third octave *C* to fifth octave *A*), tensions lower than 8 lbs cause intonation problems, are prone to buzzes and rattles, and fall at the beginning of the stretch/elasticity curve. Tensions above 22 pounds exert too much pressure for banjo bridge systems, are prone to string breakage before the desired pitch is reached, and are at the end of the stretch/elasticity curve.

- Note the difference in tensions for the Plectrum's *C* and the Tenor's *C*. This is due to the difference in fretting scale lengths of 26" and 22-3/4", respectively.

- Information is provided for the composition of wound strings. Note that in some cases the size of the core wire increases while the wrapped wire stays the same.

- Much needs to be said about those strings that are directly over a bridge foot and those which are over a bridge arch. Note the 5-string "RB" example set above. It properly has the three strings with the least tension directly over a bridge foot and those with the greatest tension directly over a bridge arch. This careful positioning of string tensions helps to modulate the various strings' amplitudes relative to their direct and indirect routes to the soundboard (head). For more on this subject, see *Chapter 5, Bridges.*

- Down pressure at the bridge and bridge height are important subjects relative to string pressure and are dealt with in detail in *Chapter 5, Bridges.*

- For more information about selecting the right gauges, see "Gauge Selection" in the following section on "Improvements You Can Make."

BRANDS

Without going into great detail, there is only a handful of string manufacturers in the United States, yet there are several hundred labels. This is not a drawback; in fact, it is quite a benefit. That small handful of manufacturers have the skill, materials, experience, machinery, marketing wisdom, and technical resources available to them to provide the very best musical strings we have ever known. The broad spectrum of private labelers work hand-in-hand with them to select and package various gauges and wrap/core combinations to offer a wide array of string sets and satisfy everyone's tastes and needs.

Over the years, I've heard musicians comment on how they love Brand X strings but hate Brand Y strings, never realizing that (in their examples) Brand Y made both sets. If the reference was to the gauge selection, I could understand the comments, but when directed towards string life, feel, or brightness, it always makes me chuckle.

CHENILLE VS PLAIN

Most loop-end banjo strings are manufactured with a felt-like finish called "chenille" around the end of the string. This desirable protective covering was intended to eliminate unwanted noises in the tailpiece and to reduce the possibility of errant string ends from catching the artist's shirt sleeve.

Octave 1	C	C#	D	D#	E	F	F#	G	G#	A	A#	B
Frequency	32.70	34.65	36.71	38.89	41.20	43.65	46.25	49.00	51.91	55.00	58.27	61.74
Octave 2	C	C#	D	D#	E	F	F#	G	G#	A	A#	B
Frequency	65.41	69.30	73.42	77.78	82.41	87.31	92.50	98.00	103.83	110.00	116.54	123.47
Octave 3	C	C#	D	D#	E	F	F#	G	G#	A	A#	B
Frequency	130.82	138.59	146.83	155.57	164.82	174.62	185.00	196.00	207.65	220.00	233.08	246.94
Octave 4	C	C#	D	D#	E	F	F#	G	G#	A	A#	B
Frequency	261.63	277.18	293.66	311.13	329.63	349.23	369.99	392.00	415.30	440.00	466.16	493.88
Octave 5	C	C#	D	D#	E	F	F#	G	G#	A	A#	B
Frequency	523.26	554.36	587.32	622.26	659.26	698.46	739.98	784.00	830.60	880.00	932.32	987.76
Octave 6	C	C#	D	D#	E	F	F#	G	G#	A	A#	B
Frequency	1046.52	1108.72	1174.64	1244.52	1318.52	1396.92	1479.96	1568.00	1661.20	1760.00	1864.64	1975.52
Octave 7	C	C#	D	D#	E	F	F#	G	G#	A	A#	B
Frequency	2093.04	2217.44	2349.28	2489.04	2637.04	2793.84	2959.92	3136.00	3322.40	3520.00	3729.28	3951.04

Fig. 8-6. This chart indicates seven octaves of notes and corresponding frequencies based on the *A440* (fourth octave A) concert pitch. The frequencies are in Hz (cycles per second).

BALL-END VS LOOP-END

This is always an oddity, especially for the banjo, as we have found tailpieces made to accommodate either ball-end or loop-end, or both. Strings were first sold as plain wire for the artist to loop. Then, the machine looping was made available. The ball-end followed, and tailpieces were made to accommodate both terminations.

FREQUENCIES OF MUSICAL STRINGS

If string frequencies interest you, Fig 8-6 is a table of the frequencies of each note in a scale which is predicated on *A440*.

OXIDATION

Strings will oxidize (rust) if not used, and therefore should be cleaned to remove any moisture before you put the instrument away. (A good reason to carry a string cleaning cloth in your case.) Some string manufacturers apply various coatings over wound strings, especially bronze wound guitar strings, to protect the brightness of the string as it sits on the store shelf.

LIFE OF THE WOUND STRING

Heavily played strings will break — especially the wraps on the wound strings — and there's just no way to get away from it. The wrap wires are prone to breakage from being constantly hammered to and vibrated against the frets. These broken wraps will cause unwanted buzzes and will cause the string to sound dull. (They'll also cut into your calluses.) Change them right away.

Improvements You Can Make

1. Gauge Selection. There is really nothing you can do to improve the strings themselves, but you can benefit from the string tension charts when buying new strings. Experiment with various gauges, even if it means changing just one string in your set to suit your playing feel.

2. Location of Attack. Experiment with various positions of attacking (picking) the strings. Playing near the bridge excites the higher numbered partials and imparts a brighter, snappier tone. Further from the bridge excites the lower numbered partials and delivers a warmer, more mellow tone.

3. Method of Attack. Different materials and weights of fingerpicks and flat picks impart a totally different tone — again an issue relative to order and amplitude of partials.

Maintenance Tips

1) Rusted strings should be replaced immediately as they are prone to breakage and possible personal injury.

2) Change strings often. Because they are tightened to pitch, strings lose their brightness and elasticity even without playing. With normal playing, it's a good idea to change them once every three to four months. If you play professionally, you will probably increase the schedule because new strings are brighter and less prone to breakage.

3) Carry a cleaning cloth in the case and clean the strings regularly.

4) Many musicians extol the virtues of boiling strings to renew their life. While the stories border on "fairy tales," there is some truth to boiling *wound* strings to rid them of natural oils that weigh them down and reduce their brightness. As with the stories of de-tensioning strings before putting the instrument away, in the long run, it's best to just work on a regular schedule of replacing exhausted strings with a fresh new pair.

5) Be sure to carry at least one extra set in your case.

Tuning the Assembly

Enter Merlin's tent where you will learn the secrets of perfecting the banjo's voice.

In the previous chapters, I provided tips that were somewhat technical, yet practical enough for you to pursue in your efforts to improve your banjo. The real mystique in setting up the banjo begins here. This is that aspect of instrument adjustment, construction, and repair that requires you to listen and focus a bit more intensely. And, this is the step that makes the difference between an exciting vibrant instrument and one that is just run-of-the-mill.

The "mystique" is centered around the magic of "tap tuning," and more specifically, the art of tuning the instrument by exciting the air chamber to vibrate, and then making adjustments to its cubic volume, stiffness, and aperture sizes.

As with any musical instrument, the body or air chamber makes several important contributions: a) it provides a chamber whose compression and rarefaction affects the surrounding air, b) it provides surfaces whose movement affects the surrounding air, c) it is comprised of parts each tuned to various pitches whose sum total comprises a specific chord which produces the associated "tone color," and d) it is tuned to a pitch which is heard as part of the whole tone or sound of the instrument which, in turn, makes up the character of that instrument.

Reread sentence "d)" above. It is a very important element to consider. Let's look at these four points one at a time.

COMPRESSION AND RAREFACTION

As described in *Chapter 2, How It Works*, the banjo — and similar instruments, for that matter — is basically an air pump. Here's the sequence of events that occurs in the production of sound: the strings are excited by the musician's picking or bowing, the string's energy drives the bridge, the bridge causes the soundboard (head) to move up and down (in various patterns), the soundboard movement causes compression and rarefaction inside the body (and some compression and rarefaction from the outside surface of the head), changes in pressure are driven through the opening between the bottom of the rim and the inside face of the resonator and then through the openings in the resonator flange, surrounding air is caused to move in sympathy, and finally we hear the banjo! Of course, it all happens in a fraction of a second.

Unlike the banjo's cousins in the mandolin, violin, and guitar families, which have both soundboards and backboards, only the soundboard (head) is active on the banjo. While some higher frequencies emanate from the back of the curved resonator and do contribute to the overall tone, its shape precludes it from having powerful vibrational modes. The resonator's primary function is to serve as a reflector sending sound away from the performer, out through the apertures in the resonator flange, as well as back into the banjo body. The resonator does need to be stiff and well made so that it does not damp any vibrations, especially when held against the performer's chest. As you will soon learn, the resonator makes enough of a contribution to the overall sound that we have to damp it to prevent it from vibrating when tuning the air chamber.

At the highest level, resonators can be tuned in manufacture. However, resonator tuning is usually regarded as an unnecessary and fruitless step by most makers.

SURFACES WHICH CONTACT SURROUNDING AIR

The only sounding board (i.e. soundboard or backboard) on a banjo is its head. As discussed in the previous paragraph, the shape of the resonator renders it useless as a sound producing backboard, although the pitch to which it is tuned (a matter of its stiffness) does contribute to the whole sound of the instrument.

As the head vibrates, it creates regions of compression and rarefaction (the opposite of compression). About 75% of the banjo's effective power is produced *inside* the air chamber, with the remaining 25% still generated from the outer surface of the head.

The changes in pressure (measured in decibels or "dB") occurring at the *outer* surface of the banjo head, project sounds forward in the absence of the contribution from the air chamber. The changes in pressure coming from the apertures in the resonator flange carry with it the tonal contribution of the air chamber, resonator, pot assembly, and so on.

PARTS TUNED TO A PITCH

Each discrete part of the banjo has a resonant frequency of its own. The resonator when held and tapped produces a tone. The head is tuned to a pitch. The pot assembly has a pitch of its own. The air chamber (more specifically, its space or cubic volume) has its own resonant frequency. Each of these components must be tuned to be in harmony with each other to complement the sound of the banjo.

The opening or space between the bottom of the rim and the inside face of the resonator is the "effective aperture." This is the opening that actually tunes the air chamber. This space acts very much like the "*f*" holes in the mandolin and violin families, and the round hole in flattop guitars.

When all parts of the instrument are put together, they become what acoustical engineers call a "coupled system," the separate pitches of which contribute to the whole tonal quality of the instrument — basically the various resonant frequencies of all of the instrument's parts taken as a whole. This is what gives any one instrument its particular *tambre* or *color*. Here's a simplified example: Let's say we have a banjo with a head tuned to a *C*, an air chamber tuned to an *E*, and a resonator tuned to a *G*. Those three notes — assuming for a moment that they will not change when we put the instrument together — will produce a *C*, *E*, *G*, in varying intensities based on the stiffness and dynamic contribution of each part, forming a *C* chord. Most importantly, that resonant *C*-chord sound of the body will be present along with every note we play, and will be that element which contributes to the instrument's overall tambre or color.

If you're wondering whether the body's tuning would affect how the instrument sounds — bright, mellow, warm, happy, sad — and those other qualities that we attribute to chords and keys — *C* being *bright* and *formal*, *E* being *warm* and *mellow*, and so on — you're right! The key to the banjo's dynamics, mood, and color comes from properly tuning its parts.

There is a counterpoint to this discussion: It is preferable to find notes that while still part of the *A440* standard, are

also notes *not* common to the keys we play in. For example, you will learn that *D#* is one of the notes recommended for tuning the head on a flattop banjo, because *D#* is not a note that would have common occurrence while playing in the somewhat standard keys of *G*, *A*, *C*, and *D*. (While it does occur as the third in the key of *B*, its occurrence is less common than a *G*, for example. And yes, I do recognize that we might hit the *D#* when playing melodically.) If the head were to be tuned to a *G* and we played a *G* or *G* chord, the head would resonate in sympathy with the played note and the instrument would be excessively bright for that note or chord. This is similar to the problem of "wolf notes" associated with sympathetic vibrations caused in the bowed viol family instruments. Suffice it to say, it is optimal to choose notes when "tuning" an instrument that are *less* common to our playing styles but still part of the *A440* standard. Most importantly, these parts must be tuned to a specific note and not tuned sharp or flat.

AIR CHAMBER TUNED TO A PITCH

In the late 1800s, a highly respected scientist named Hermann Helmholz (1821 – 1894) discovered the relationship between the size of air chambers and their resonant frequencies. He experimented with the note or pitch that various sized chambers would produce (their "resonant frequencies") when excited using various methods (tapped, picked, bowed, or air blown across their apertures). From his studies, he found that large chambers produced low notes and small ones produced high notes, as may seem common to us when we think of low notes of the bass viols compared to treble qualities of the violins.

Another important discovery was that round chambers — particularly spherical (ball-shaped) ones — resonated better than those with flatted facing sides (box-shaped). This feature explains the banjo's unique liveliness due to its rounded walls, curved resonator (with the exception of Gibson's Top Tension models, which boasted a resonator with a flat inside face), and singular flatted side (the head).

THE CRITICAL DISCOVERY

Continuing his studies, Helmholz learned that for every chamber size there was an ideally sized aperture (opening) which provided maximum amplitude of the resonant frequency. This is important, so let me rephrase it: Each air chamber or space has a resonant frequency relative to its size, and each space has an aperture or opening which optimally tunes that space. We know this because, for example, when we blow across the mouth of a soda bottle, we hear a note which is the resonant frequency of the space in the bottle. If we fill the bottle with water (making the space smaller), and blow across the mouth of the bottle, the pitch increases. And, somewhere during the filling process, we arrive at a point where the bottle, with its fixed-size opening, vibrates more loudly than at any other point — a point at which we discover the optimum relationship between the size of the air chamber and the size of the aperture. But what happens when we change the size of the opening to the bottle (a test that is difficult to perform with glass bottles)? In reality, if we could make the opening to the soda bottle larger, the pitch would increase, if we could make it smaller the pitch would drop, and, somewhere in the middle, the bottle resonates wildly as we achieve the "maximum amplitude" when we find an opening which is the ideal size for the cubic volume of that air chamber. This relationship is what we seek in tuning the air chamber of musical instruments.

TUNING MUSICAL INSTRUMENTS

Finally, we come to the art of tuning the resonant frequencies of the various components of the air chamber — not just the space, but the elements that comprise or contain the space. While Helmholtz devoted his attention to the cubic volume of the space and to the size of the aperture, it was artisans like Stradivarius, Guarneri, Amati and others who focused on the contribution of the walls of the air chambers; the soundboard, backboard, and ribs. They pondered the merits of tuning the stiffness of these elements to specific notes to enhance the quality of the resonant space and make it a rich tone producer, as well.

Thus we enter the magic of tuning an instrument body which includes: tuning the cavity or air chamber, tuning the apertures, and adjusting the stiffness of the soundboard (head), backboard (resonator), and sides (rim). The real mystique is manifest in the art of "tap tuning," which is the technique of tapping on an object to excite its parts or the air within to determine the note to which it is tuned, and then adjusting the stiffness or size of that object to alter its tuning, if needed.

Tap Tuning
The foregoing is the "tap tuning" part we hear so much about in the building and repair of musical instruments. Adjusting the body size, getting the apertures or openings (like "*f*" holes) to be just the right size for the body size, and adjusting the stiffness of the soundboard and braces (in the case of the banjo, the tightness of the head), are just some of the things we do to *tune* the chamber of the instrument and make it a highly sensitive tone-producing system.

Changing the Apertures
As in the previous example of the soda bottle, if we make "*f*" holes or soundholes larger, we raise the pitch of the air chamber, and if we make them smaller we lower the pitch. On the banjo, the soundhole or effective aperture is that space between the bottom of the rim and the inside face of the resonator (Fig. 9-1). The larger that space is, the higher the pitch of the air chamber becomes, until we finally reach a size which destroys or invalidates the space as an air chamber and loses any sign of a resonant frequency. At this point, all compression and rarefaction

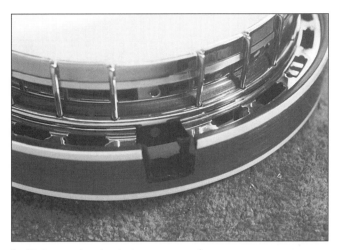

Fig. 9-1. Removing the neck makes it easy to measure the aperture.

happens equally on both sides of the soundboard (head), and without the air chamber playing a role, we get the sound and dynamics associated with an open-back banjo.

As the aperture gets smaller, the pitch drops. As we keep closing the aperture, getting the rim closer to the resonator, we reach a point where there is too much restriction for compression and rarefaction to be effective. As the aperture keeps closing, we cut off the air chamber from the surrounding air and can only generate sound pressure (waves of compression and rarefaction) from the front surface of the banjo's soundboard (head). At this point, the instrument sounds basically "dead" and powerless.

HEARING THE TAPPED TONES

One part of the magic is being able to hear the tapped tone. What does it sound like? Is it bell-like? Is it like a note from the strings? Well, it's easier for you to test than for me to describe. Lay the banjo on a soft padded chair or couch to protect the resonator, and remove the screws that hold the resonator in place. Grab the banjo neck and slowly pull the banjo from the resonator at an angle as if there were a hinge holding the tailpiece to the resonator. As you do this, tap on the head and listen to the pitch change as you raise and lower the banjo from its resonator.

You are changing two things as you do this: the size of the effective aperture (the space between the rim and the resonator), and the size of the air chamber (obviously, you make the space between the pot assembly and the resonator larger as you lift up on the banjo neck).

Damp the strings with your hand to prevent them from vibrating. Listen to the tone change, again. At first, it's hard to distinguish the note from the "tap" — listen carefully. The pitch change will become quickly obvious. You can make the job easier if you use a special tapping hammer.

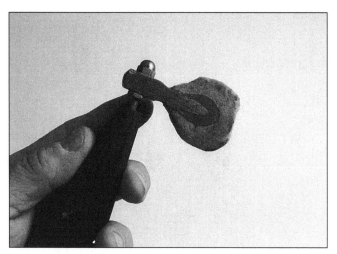

Fig. 9-2. A tapping tool can be made from a discarded piano key hammer. Or, you can tape a piece of felt or soft rubber to the face of a small hammer.

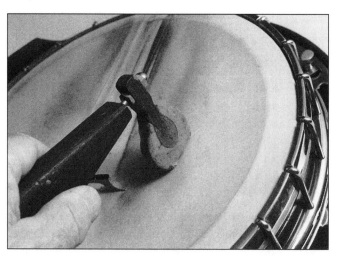

Fig. 9-3. Hold the banjo upright so that you hear the sound directly in front of you. Tap to the right of the bridge.

TUNING TOOLS TO TAP WITH

Tapping with the finger will work for this test, but for reliable tuning, and so that you do not excite any of the higher partials (which the pointed end of your finger will do), you should use a padded tapping tool. Fig. 9-2 shows a tapping hammer I made about 30 years ago and have been using ever since (the face has flattened a bit from usage). I took a piano hammer and bolted it to a rosewood handle (the rosewood was an extravagance on my part, any piece of wood will do). You can also make a good tapping hammer by wrapping a rag over the face of a small hammer. Whatever you come up with, be sure the face is made of soft material and is wider than the end of your finger.

TELL THE STRINGS TO BE QUIET

After you have experimented a bit and are ready to make your adjustments, take a piece of felt, or cloth, and weave it through the strings at the 12th fret or so. The exact location is not critical, but you want to damp the strings vibrations so they don't interfere with tuning the air chamber. Place some fabric or tissue paper under the tailpiece cover to damp it. Also, put a small piece of cloth under the tailpiece to damp it and prevent it from vibrating.

WHERE TO TAP

This is a really strange phenomenon, and without going into a great deal of background, if you tap your hammer on the head (with the assembly closed) you'll hear the resonant frequency of the air chamber. If you tap the hammer on the bridge, you'll hear the resonant frequency of the soundboard (head). (Make sure the strings are damped.)

Anyway, for checking the pitch of the head, do it with the pot assembly off of the resonator. Place the tailpiece end of the pot assembly against your stomach with the neck extending away from you. Tap halfway between the bridge and the tone chamber. Close your eyes and listen.

For checking the pitch of the air chamber, follow the previous instructions about lifting the pot assembly in and out of the resonator. Again, tap the head halfway between the bridge and the tone chamber.

FINDING THE RIGHT PITCH

I use either a piano or a stroboscopic (analog) tuner as reference for the notes I hear when tap tuning. Some digital tuners have a fast response curve and will read and display the tapped notes, others do not. The older stroboscopic tuners have a much slower response curve and display the note for a longer period of time. If you use another instrument as a reference, do your tapping, hum the note you hear, and then find the note on the other instrument. A little practice will make you an expert!

NOTE

As you lower the banjo into the resonator, determine if the richness or fullness of the tapped tone gets muted to where you can no longer hear the note of the air chamber, but hear a "thud" instead. Should this occur, it is an indication that the bottom edge of the rim is getting too close to the inside face of the resonator and, in effect, closing the aperture too far. If this happens, be sure to consult section "3. Major Air Chamber Tuning Corrections" under "Improvements You Can Make."

STRINGS MUST BE AT PITCH

Before making any adjustments, bring the strings up to pitch. Use a tuner to be sure they are to concert pitch (based on *A440*). Having the strings at pitch is important because the string tension affects the amount of down pressure at the bridge which, in turn, adds pressure to the head and alters the pitch to which it is tuned. Therefore, tune the head to pitch *after* the strings are tuned to pitch.

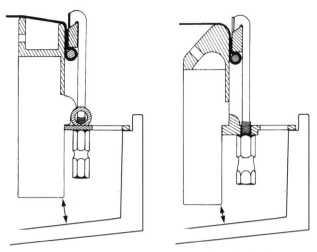

Fig. 9-4. The aperture on the one-piece flange banjo is (typically) smaller than the aperture on the tube-and-plate banjo. With slight modifications, both air chambers can both be tuned to the correct pitch.

Fig. 9-5. With both pots sitting on a flat surface, it is easy to see that the one-piece flange (left) is higher than the tube-and-plate flange. This results in a lower rim position when the pot is placed in the resonator.

WHAT IF THE PARTS CANNOT BE TUNED TO A RECOMMENDED PITCH?

If you cannot adjust your banjo to the specific notes provided here, at the very least tune them to a note which is part of the *A440* scale. It is critically important that all notes emitted from your banjo are part of the same tuning standard or scale. If, for example, you attempt to tune the head to a *G392*, but it ends up a few cents flat (a cent is one hundredth of a semitone) so that it is actually a *G390*, for example, and you have a *G* string on your banjo tuned to a perfect *G392*, then you will hear very unpleasant "beats" of two cycles per second, which is the difference between the two notes *(392Hz – 390Hz = 2Hz)*.

ONE-PIECE FLANGE VS TUBE-AND-PLATE GIBSON-TYPE INSTRUMENTS

There is a major difference between one-piece and tube-and-plate flange instruments that affects their tone. The rim heights, including tone chambers, of both instruments are typically very close to the same. However, due to the architecture of the two different flanging systems, the bottom of the one-piece flange ends up being positioned about 5/16" higher on the rim than the tube-and-plate flange (Fig. 9-5). This means that when the pot assembly of one-piece flange instruments is set into the resonator, the bottom of the rim will come closer to the resonator, causing the aperture to be about 5/16" smaller than on tube-and-plate models.

DIFFERENCES IN CONSTRUCTION

Banjos are made of machined wooden parts that are hand sanded and hand fitted, and no two banjos of the same model have the same measurements when assembled. This calls for the need to adjust the aperture and to custom tune each instrument.

ONE LAST THING

You are entering a process in which tuning one element will have an affect on another element, and you may have to go through the process a minimum of two or three times until you arrive at the optimum tuning. For example, you may find that you tune the head and change the bridge height. Then you determine that the new height and resultant down pressure retunes the head, so you need to retune the head, and so on. Be patient!

READY, SET, GO!

Now, armed with the information from this and previous chapters, you are ready to embark on the final changes and adjustments to your banjo.

Improvements You Can Make

1. Head Tuning. (Note: Complete this step *before* tuning the air chamber.) The head is tuned to pitch by tightening the bracket nuts. Make sure to apply equal tension to each and every nut as you go around the rim. Here are the optimum tunings for archtop and flattop banjos. The difference in tuning is due to the difference in the areas (i.e. active diameters of 9.5" vs 11") of the respective heads:

Archtop: *E,* ***F,*** *or F#*

Flattop: *D,* ***D#,*** *E*

NOTES

1) The notes in bold face type are the preferred tunings.

2) Tightening the bracket nuts increases the pitch, loosening them lowers the pitch.

3) Technically, the tension should be the same for both the archtop and flattop heads at these tunings. The archtop has a surface area of 29.85 square inches and the flattop has an area of 34.54 square inches. If we apply the "12th root of 2" principle that is

Fig. 9-6. If a small change is needed, the flange can be raised by gluing a shim of black plastic to the resonator lip. (White material was shown here for photographic purposes.)

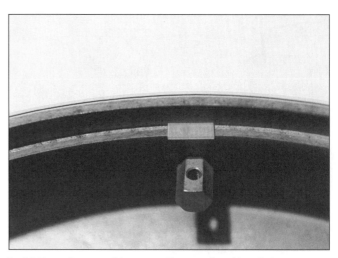

Fig. 9-7. To raise the pot out of the resonator (thus raising the pitch), single shim pieces can be glued to the resonator above the studs.

used for musical scale calculations, the difference between the areas of those two heads is mathematically two half steps apart. Thus, the scientific and empirical evaluations appear to concur.

2. Air Chamber Tuning. (Note: Complete this step only *after* tuning the head in step #1, above.) If you are fortunate enough to have your instrument set up close to perfect at the outset, you should be able to tune the air chamber easily. For this test, *place the banjo in its case* to damp the resonator.

NOTE

Tuning the head while the resonator is attached and the banjo is held out of the case could raise the pitch of the air chamber as much as a whole tone. We want to tune the air chamber with the resonator's back damped (prevented from vibrating), so for this test, the banjo should be in its case.

Using the technique previously described, raise and lower the pot assembly into the resonator as you tap. You should be able to determine the resonant frequency of the air chamber. For Gibson banjos this should be:

Archtop, tube-and-plate: *C* or ***C#***

Archtop, one-piece flange: *C* or ***C#***

Flattop, tube-and-plate: *A* or ***A#***

Flattop, one-piece flange: *A* or ***A#***

NOTES

1) The notes in bold face type are the preferred tunings.

2) One-piece flange instruments can be adjusted a full semitone higher if the pot assembly is sufficiently raised. This would be preferred since it would bring the instruments to a C# or A#, respectively.

Effective aperture: Just for reference, or if you have trouble hearing the tapped tone and decide to proceed by measurements alone, a reliable starting point for the aperture should be 1/2". However, bear in mind that this is an approximate measurement and does not "tune" your banjo, per se.

If the tuning is *slightly* flat but the tap-tone is "full": You can raise the pitch by raising the pot assembly out of the resonator, making the effective aperture slightly larger. This is the easiest change and there are two simple ways to accomplish this: 1) glue a minimum of six thin wood or plastic curved shims, evenly spaced around the underside of the flange, 2) glue a long thin strip of black binding plastic or similar material to the top of the resonator lip. Each of these methods will raise the pot assembly out of the resonator and will be cosmetically pleasing. You may have to glue two or three strips on top of each other (for either method) until you arrive at the correct pitch. The pitch will change quickly with very little change in height.

NOTE

If your banjo is designed such that the angle brackets — not the flange — are resting on the lip, affix the shims to the underside of the brackets.

You can easily test the adjustment before gluing anything to the banjo by merely shimming up the flange (where it contacts the resonator) and re-attaching the resonator. If you are happy with the results, make the change permanent.

NOTE

To facilitate gluing a long thin strip onto the resonator's lip, use contact cement. Bend the strip into a circle first to aid the installation process. Be sure to mask off any area of the resonator that should not receive cement. With contact cement, you'll be able to quickly apply the thin strip to the curved resonator notch. Follow instructions for proper usage on the cement can.

If the tuning is flat and the tapped tone is a dull "thud": This suggests that the effective aperture is too small (a measurement which is probably less than 3/8"). The pot assembly may have be raised more than is feasible with shims as described in the previous section. One satisfactory method for raising the pot assembly is to move the resonator brackets outboard so that they rest on the resonator lip, rather than the flange resting on the lip. As shown in

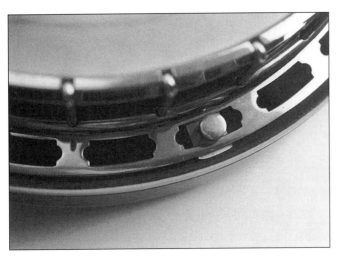

Fig. 9-8. This 1926 tube-and-plate instrument has the rim brackets resting on the resonator's lip. (The flange is not touching the rim.) It was tuned to a perfect C# and required no adjustment.

Fig. 9-9. The pot assembly on this 1960s RB250 had to be raised almost 1/4" to achieve the correct tuning. Blocks were added (with longer screws) behind each angle bracket, thus allowing the brackets to rest on the resonator lip to raise the flange.

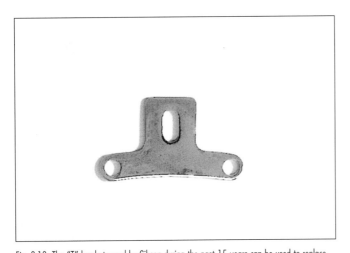

Fig. 9-10. The "T" brackets used by Gibson during the past 15 years can be used to replace angle brackets on one-piece flange banjos. (See. Fig. 9-11)

Fig. 9-11. Only a 3/16" change was required on this banjo. "T" brackets replaced the conventional angle brackets and extended far enough to sit on the resonator lip to raise the pot.

Fig. 9-8, the brackets on early Gibson banjos rested on the resonator lip holding the flange above it. Fig. 9-9 shows how the brackets were moved out on a 1960 RB-250 to raise the pot assembly while tuning this instrument. An alternative method is to purchase or fabricate some of the stamped brackets (Fig. 9-10) Gibson used in the 1980s on tube-and-plate models. These extend to the edge of the resonator and sit on the resonator lip. If used with one-piece flanges, they effectively raise the pot assembly about 1/4" (Fig. 9-11). They can be bent for various heights to precisely tune the air chamber.

NOTE

For this instrument, the initial affective aperture was about 3/16" too small. The tuning process called for the use of these stamped flanges and resulted in exceptional results. A fourth bracket was added since banjos of this period featured only three brackets; four are preferred.

If additional tuning needs to be performed, and the pot assembly needs to be either raised or lowered, the brackets can be bent or shimmed to make the final adjustment.

NOTE

The above steps may seem contradictory. You have learned that making the air chamber larger (moving the pot assembly out of the resonator) lowers its resonant frequency. You have also learned that increasing the size of the aperture (also by moving the pot assembly out of the resonator) raises the resonant frequency. Contradiction? Yes, and no. Both of these statements are true. The most important part of this process is to find an aperture that tunes the space. Go for the tuning! Your banjo will become "alive" when you reach the correct adjustment and the positive results will become quickly evident.

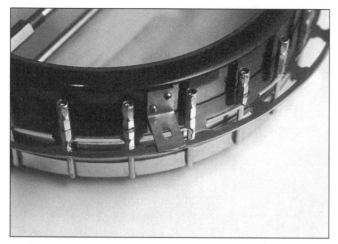

Fig. 9-12. These long angle brackets were used on early Gibson instruments and extended to the resonator lip. (See. Fig. 9-8.)

Fig. 9-13. If the pot has to be lowered (to lower the pitch) and the banjo has "T" brackets, replace them with shortened angle brackets. These replacement brackets were installed directly over the "T" brackets to insure alignment before the "T" brackets were removed.

Fig. 9-14. With the "T" bracket removed, the shortened angle bracket cleared the resonator and allowed this pot to drop 1/8" for accurate tuning.

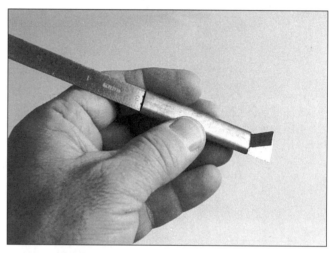

Fig. 9-15. A simple measuring tool can be made by forming a piece of thin copper tubing over a machinist's rule. The protruding lip is used to measure to the bottom of the rim.

If the tuning is *slightly* sharp: Closing the aperture is a bit more difficult than opening it and is also a less common occurrence. If your banjo is equipped with resonator brackets that rest on the resonator lip, they can be either cut shorter or replaced with standard angle brackets that come short of the resonator lip. In either case, this change will allow the flange to rest on the resonator lip, thus moving the pot assembly further into the resonator cavity and closing the aperture.

If the flange is resting on the resonator lip such that you cannot lower the pot assembly any further into the resonator, you can add material to the bottom of the rim — this is much easier than cutting into the resonator lip. You can test how much is needed by cutting rings of plastic or hard cardboard and temporarily taping them to the bottom of the rim. Strange as this may sound, the cardboard will work effectively to alter the tuning. Add material until you arrive at the proper note. Playing the instrument for a while and listening to the improvement will tell you

whether it is worth it for you to make a permanent addition to the bottom of the rim. Should you choose to make the change, you can add a layer of ebony, maple, celluloid, or any other dense, hard material of your choice. You should consider allowing an experienced luthier to make this adjustment for you since the process will require the rim to be refinished. (See machining details in the next section.)

3. Major Air Chamber Tuning Corrections. Occasionally we encounter instruments that need major adjustments to the depth of the rim, including cutting down or building up its height. This is especially a problem with one-piece flange instruments whose higher positioning of the flange (relative to the tube-and-plate models) forces the rim to be positioned lower in the resonator.

First, you must measure the space (effective aperture) between the bottom of the rim and the inside face of the resonator. There are two methods to do this: 1) Unstring the instrument, remove the neck, reinstall the resonator,

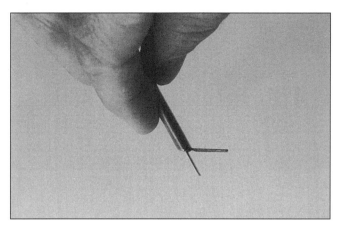

Fig. 9-16. Here's a side view of the measuring tool in Fig. 9-15: the ruler contacts the bottom of the resonator, and the bent lip on the tube touches the bottom of the rim.

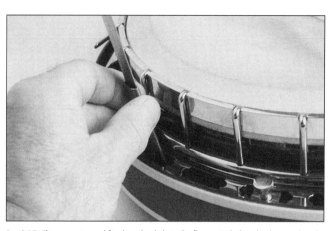

Fig. 9-17. The measuring tool fits through a hole in the flange. Push the ruler down and read the measurement that aligns with the top of the tube. Remove the tool and slide the ruler up flush with the bottom of the tube. Reread the measurement. The difference in the two measurements is the size of the aperture.

and measure the space between the resonator and bottom edge of the rim. 2) Fabricate a measurement tool as shown in Fig. 9-15 which will enable you to measure the space without dismantling the instrument. For both archtop and flattop (Gibson) banjos this space should be between 7/16" and 1/2" (the actual size dependent on final tuning) and should be no less than 1/4" or more than 9/16". For reference, the aperture in the 1926 Gibson tube-and-plate archtop shown in Fig. 9-8 was 1/2", which tuned the air chamber to a *C#* with its resonator damped (the instrument in its case).

Check the rim height: If the space is less than 1/4", remove the resonator and measure the rim height from the bottommost portion of the rim to the inside of the head. For both archtop and flattop (Gibson) banjos this should be 2-7/8". If the measurement is greater or less than 1/8", you must modify the rim. To do this, the instrument must be disassembled and the rim either built up or cut down, followed by refinishing the rim.

Maintenance Tip

Many things can change that alter the head and air chamber tuning. Check the tunings on the same cycle with your string changes. Make sure you check the tunings with the strings up to pitch.

Amplification

Now that you have modified your banjo so that it sounds great to your ears, the next test is: "how does it sound when amplified?" After all, for those of you who play professionally, whether as full-time or part-time musicians, getting that banjo to work on stage is where it counts.

To learn about amplification, I thought it would be fun to step away from my workbench for one chapter and turn the spotlight on the man who carved a path to our homes and hearts with his magical recordings. It was more than technique and style that made Earl Scruggs' banjo playing so unique. His knowledge of *how* to amplify and record the banjo made the difference. So, it is with great pleasure that I turn the pen over to Earl and give him a warm thanks for his contribution to this text.

◄ BY EARL SCRUGGS ►

When Roger asked me to describe some of my techniques to amplify the banjo, I wasn't quite sure where to start. So, before talking about amplification, I think the most important thing for me to point out is that if I had my choice, I'd prefer the banjo not to be amplified. That is, its natural sound, the full rich sound of the banjo without being amplified, is what I enjoy the most. I have also never heard a banjo recorded that sounds as true as one that is totally acoustic right next to you. And, this is what I look for when I am being amplified — I want the amplified sound of the banjo to sound as acoustic as possible.

Amplification for me has always been a necessity more than a desire. As I began to play professionally, that brought me to perform on a stage with other musicians, and that meant that I needed to be heard by everyone in the audience along with the rest of the band. Amplification was used to make us more easily heard, not "amplified." That may sound like a slim difference, but I guess you would say it is a philosophical point.

I'd often work with a sound man, I guess they're called sound engineers today, and they'd ask, "do you want more treble?" or "do you want more bass?" and I'd say, "come down here and listen to this banjo for a few minutes." I wanted them to hear it as an acoustic instrument so they could match that sound. If I began to tell them more this or that, I'm not sure if we'd ever make it right. Usually, when they'd stop to listen to the acoustic instrument, they would be able to go back and get it to come out right through the speakers.

Years ago, the band used to work into one microphone, and that meant that each of us would have to move around a lot in time to get to the mike for our breaks. In some ways, I think it was interesting for the audience to watch us work that way. But it also meant that our timing had to be perfect. One mike also meant that we had to play a little bit louder when doing backup, because we couldn't always get close enough to work into the mike.

After that, we began to use a few mikes, but we still didn't use as many mikes as we do today. By that I mean, today each of us have one mike for voice and another for our instruments. Back then, two or sometimes three of us would have to share one instrument mike to play into. I think that kind of amplification worked out better than just working against a monitor the way we do today. When you are playing face to face with someone else, it's better than working into a monitor because you have the advantage of hearing each other, blending into each other, working the dynamics off each other, and so on.

By the time each of us got to have our own mikes we also used monitors, so you did have the advantage of hearing yourself. If the monitor is balanced properly, you can get a good idea of how you sound along with everyone else. And this brings up another important point. You need to have someone work the board for you and stay with it all the way through the performance. The sound engineer must take into account how the sound works in a room, because the acoustics of the room might be very different from just what you are hearing in the monitor. He's got to balance for the *room* as well as giving you a good idea in your monitor of how you sound.

Fig. 10-1. Of the many pickups Earl has tried, he has favored both the Acoustic-Plus (Gerald Jones, Dallas TX) and Barcus Berry (Huntington Beach, CA) pickups. They are mounted on a special bracket which is attached to the coordinator rods.

Fig. 10-2. Pickup position is important. Earl prefers the pickup to be about one inch from the bridge, towards the tailpiece.

Fig. 10-3. Earl uses a phono plug going into a bracket just below the tailpiece so he can disconnect the wire quickly when moving off stage. The wire feeds back and out of the way of his feet.

When the (The Earl Scruggs) Revue was together (featuring Earl and his sons Randy, Gary, and Steve) we were primarily a plugged-in band and had a full set of drums, and if I wanted to be heard, I had to work amplified. I used both an inside pickup as well as working into the microphone. Using a pickup gives you consistency. By that I mean, you don't have to worry about how close you are to the mike or whether you are facing it properly — the banjo is always the same because the pickup is in a fixed position. With a pickup, you are at the mercy of your sound man and you have to trust him, and he has to know your playing style. The drawback with a pickup is that it is always "hot" and you can't use phrasing; that is, the dynamics of pulling back from the microphone or working up closer to it like you can when just working with a mike. Without the pickup, you can use phrasing and work against the mike.

In the studio, we use headphones instead of a monitor. It's a bit more personal that way — you can hear everything much better without any outside noise, and the studio doesn't have problems of picking up any sounds from monitors. Another advantage I have in the studio is that during the past many years, almost all of my recording has been at my son Randy's studio (Scruggs Sound Studio, Nashville, TN), and he knows better than anyone else exactly what I am looking for, what my acoustic playing sounds like, and how my banjo should sound both acoustic *and* amplified. (Randy used an RCA77DZ ribbon mike for Earl's banjo on the *Circle Be Unbroken* album. Since then, Randy switched to a U67 Neumann tube condenser mike to capture the banjo.)

As far as where to position the microphone on the banjo, I've tried just about everything, and I think I've come to the conclusion that just below my (right) hand and facing the head is the best. I have not had good results with trying to record the sound coming from the resonator, through the holes in the flange. And, I am not satisfied with trying to record the whole banjo from, let's say, 15" inches or so back from the banjo. I think recording directly from the head is best, about 3" or 4" away from the head. Sometimes there may be a little bit of clicking noise from the picks, and this is an indication that the mike is too close to the hand and the picks. Move it away and off to one side, and the pick noise should go away.

For monitors, I don't need a dedicated one. Just as long as I can hear myself and the other members of the band, I'm satisfied. I also don't mind having the monitors on the stage floor; that works fine for me. I do listen to the monitors and pay more attention to the monitor's sound than what I might hear coming directly from the banjo.

Again, for me, the truest banjo sound is the one that I hear when I play acoustic. This is when I hear sounds from the head, from the opening in the resonator, and from the back of the resonator, and all those little extra sounds that get lost when I try to record or amplify the banjo. I'm sure that someday, they'll find a way to capture it all.

Wrap Up

Having made all the adjustments you can make, here are some closing thoughts just to keep things in perspective.

THE OPTIMUM SOUND

Is there one "optimum sound?" Probably not. I think we all hear sound differently, much in the same way we see colors differently, and taste foods differently. After all, each of us enjoys wearing different colors, and there is a wide variety of foods to satisfy an equally wide variety of tastes.

However, it is commonly held that a good sounding banjo is bright, clear, and powerful with quick attack and good sustain. Of course, it must note true and have good intonation on all strings up and down the neck. The optimum banjo has a well contained sound with no "tubby-ness" or echoes. The neck is solid and well connected, and putting slight pressure on it does not change the pitch of the instrument. The neck fits well in the hand, and the strings are easy to access and fret. Generally, the instrument is easy to play. And, it is these qualities that come from a well tuned, properly adjusted and set up instrument.

In the introduction to this text, I spoke of bluegrass musicians wanting that magical banjo that "sounded like Earl's." A great deal of the magic is in Earl Scruggs himself and more specifically, his right and left hand; how he attacks the strings, the angle and type of picks, the power in his fingers, and so on. That's at least half the magic. Having had the pleasure of jamming with him and listening to him play different banjos, somehow . . . they all sounded like "Earl's."

Don't lose sight of the fact that a critical part of the acoustical system — the devices that attack the strings — are those five little things attached to each of your hands.

INTERACTION OF ADJUSTMENTS

Undoubtedly, you will find that you make one adjustment and have to go back and remake another. Remember that you are working with a coupled system — all of the banjo's components relate to each other. After getting the right string angle, you then tune the head and air chamber, only to find that its new sensitivity leads you to a new gauge of strings, which leads you to a new bridge, which leads you to retuning the head. Chasing your tail? Not really, just getting closer to the truth! Add a little patience and everything will work out fine.

POWER-TUNING CHECKLIST

Here is a list of various aspects of power-tuning in order of their contribution to the overall sound, beginning with the most important. For more information on each topic, consult the Index for where the subject matter can be found in the text.

Head tuned to the correct pitch

Air chamber tuned to correct pitch (tuned aperture)

Sizing the air chamber

Tuning (stiffness) of resonator

Shape of resonator

Location of bridge

String angle (over bridge)

Tailpiece height behind bridge (down pressure)

Age of strings

Gauge of strings

Tone chamber fit

Bridge design (weight)

Tone chamber type (arch vs flat)

Tailpiece design (length, stiffness)

Neck heel to stretcher band contact

Flange (one-piece, tube-and-plate, shoes and plates)

Bridge height

Heads (clear or sprayed)

Thickness of head (painted coating)

Neck wood

Neck fit

Resonator wood and construction

Rim wood and construction

Truss rod adjustment*

Tuning machines (weight, mass)

Nut (material)

Coordinator rod type

Coordinator rod adjustment

Lag screws

Hooks and nuts

Stretcher band

Armrest

Thumb screws

Resonator attaching hardware

As it relates to neck stiffness and proper intonation control.

EASY-TUNING CHECKLIST

In order of ease of accomplishment (the first being the *easiest* to do), here is a listing of various aspects of power-tuning (in case you want to approach the process more slowly). For more information on each topic, consult the Index for where the subject matter can be found in the text:

Age of strings

Gauge of strings

Location of bridge

Tailpiece height behind bridge (down pressure)

Bridge height

Tailpiece design (length, stiffness)

Bridge design (weight)

Coordinator rod adjustment

Heads (clear or sprayed)

Head tuned to the correct pitch

Truss rod adjustment*

Air chamber tuned to correct pitch (tuned aperture, resonator to bottom of rim)

Thickness of head (painted coating)

String angle (over bridge)

Tone chamber fit

Tone chamber type (arch vs flat)

Resonator wood and construction

Rim wood and construction

Machines (weight, mass)

Nut (material)

Flange (one-piece, tube-and-plate, shoes and plates)

Neck wood

As it relates to neck stiffness and proper intonation control.

Index